Teacher's Book

A RESOURCE FOR PLANNING AND TEACHING

Level K WOW! Wonder of Words

Senior Authors J. David Cooper, John J. Pikulski

Authors Kathryn H. Au, Margarita Calderón, Jacqueline C. Comas, Marjorie Y. Lipson, J. Sabrina Mims, Susan E. Page, Sheila W. Valencia, MaryEllen Vogt

Consultants Dolores Malcolm, Tina Saldivar, Shane Templeton

INVITATIONS
TO LITERACY

Houghton Mifflin Company • Boston

Atlanta • Dallas • Geneva, Illinois • Palo Alto • Princeton

Acknowledgments

Grateful acknowledgment is made for permission to reprint copyrighted material as follows:

"First Snow," from *A Pocketful of Poems*, by Marie Louise Allen. Copyright © 1957 by Marie Allen Howarth. Reprinted by permission of HarperCollins Publishers.

Hunky Dory Found It, by Katie Evans, illustrated by Janet Morgan Stoeke. Text copyright © 1994 by Katie Evans. Illustrations copyright © 1994 by Janet Morgan Stoeke. Reprinted by permission of Dutton Children's Books, a division of Penguin Books USA, Inc.

I Have a Pet, by Shari Halpern. Copyright © 1994 by Shari Halpern. Reprinted by permission of Macmillan Books for Young Readers, Simon & Schuster Children's Publishing Division.

"In Downtown Philadelphia," from *Beneath a Blue Umbrella*, by Jack Prelutsky. Copyright © 1990 by Jack Prelutsky. Reprinted by permission of Greenwillow Books, a division of William Morrow and Company, Inc.

Jamaica's Find, by Juanita Havill, illustrated by Anne Sibley O'Brien. Text copyright © 1986 by Juanita Havill. Illustrations copyright © 1986 by Anne Sibley O'Brien. Reprinted by permission of Houghton Mifflin Company. All rights reserved.

"The More We Get Together," traditional.

My Big Dictionary, by the Editors of the American Heritage Dictionaries, illustrated by Pamela Cote. Copyright © 1994 by Houghton Mifflin Company. All rights reserved.

"My Bird Is Small," from *Something Sleeping in the Hall*, by Karla Kuskin. Copyright © 1985 by Karla Kuskin. Reprinted by permission of HarperCollins Publishers.

"Oh Where, Oh Where Has My Little Dog Gone?" traditional.

Snow on Snow on Snow, by Cheryl Chapman, illustrated by Synthia Saint James. Text copyright © 1994 by Cheryl Chapman. Paintings copyright © 1994 by Synthia Saint James. Reprinted by permission of Dial Books for Young Readers, a division of Penguin Books USA, Inc.

Together, by George Ella Lyon, illustrated by Vera Rosenberry. Text copyright © 1989 by George Ella Lyons. Illustrations copyright © 1989 by Vera Rosenberry. Reprinted by permission of Orchard Books, New York.

What Shall We Do When We All Go Out? a traditional song, illustrated by Shari Halpern. Text adapted by Philip H. Bailey. Copyright © 1995 by Shari Halpern. Reprinted by permission of North-South Books, Inc.

"With a Friend," by Vivian Gouled, from *Poetry Place Anthology*. Copyright © 1978 by Instructor Publications. Reprinted by permission of Vivian Gouled.

Credits

Cover photography by © Paul Barton/ The Stock Market (t); © Bill Losh/ FPG (b)

Assignment Photography

Theme: Let's Be Friends
Tracey Wheeler, pp. T13, T26, T29, T33, T57, T63, T64, T87, T89, T91, T97, T100; Tony Scarpetta, pp. T84, T86; Banta Digital Group, pp. T4, T5, T6, T7, T14, T34, T62, T63, T66, T87; Kathy Copeland, pp. T28, T33, T54, T56, T88, T96

Theme: Playful Pets
Tracey Wheeler, pp. T111, T127, T131, T154, T155, T161, T163, T184, T187, T189, T191, T195; Tony Scarpetta, pp. T157, T161; Banta Digital Group, pp. T102, T103, T104, T105, T112, T129, T132, T155, T164, T185, T187, T189; Kathy Copeland, pp. T125, T126, T127, T131, T153, T162, T163, T188, T200

Photography

Theme: Let's Be Friends
Courtesy of Houghton Mifflin Trade Books, p. T14; Courtesy of Shari Halpern, p. T34; Courtesy of Orchard Books, p. T66; © Paul Barton/The Stock Market, p. T3

Theme: Playful Pets
Courtesy of Shari Halpern, p. T112; Courtesy of Cheryl Chapman, p. T164; © Bill Losh/FPG, p. T101; Photo courtesy of Houghton Mifflin Trade Books, p. T108

Let's Be Friends

Table of Contents
THEME: Let's Be Friends

Big Books *LITERATURE FOR WHOLE CLASS AND SMALL GROUP INSTRUCTION*

by George Ella Lyon
illustrated by Vera Rosenberry

fiction

WATCH ME READ Books *PRACTICE FOR HIGH-FREQUENCY WORDS AND PHONICS SKILLS*

Each title is also available in black and white. This version includes a home activity.

Bibliography

Books for the Library Corner

 Multicultural

 Science/Health

 Math

 Social Studies

 Music

 Art

Hilda Hen's Happy Birthday
by Mary Wormell
Harcourt 1995 (32p)
Hilda Hen wonders if her farm friends really left all of the presents she finds for her.

Going for a Walk
by Beatrice Schenk de Regniers
Harper 1993 (24p)
A girl goes for a walk and finds a friend.

Best Friends
by Miriam Cohen
Macmillan 1971 (32p) also paper
Kindergarten classmates Jim and Paul realize that they are best friends.

Lizzie and Her Friend
by David Martin
Candlewick 1993 (24p)
Lizzie and a friend have fun playing with water.

A Boy, a Dog, a Frog, and a Friend
by Mercer Mayer
Puffin (32p)
A boy, his dog, and his frog go fishing and catch a turtle which becomes their friend. (Wordless)

Do You Want to Be My Friend?
by Eric Carle
Crowell 1971 (32p) also paper
A small mouse has a hard time finding a friend.

The Friend
by John Burningham
Candlewick 1994 (24p)
A boy describes the ups and downs of his friendship with Arthur.

Margaret and Margarita/Margarita y Margaret
 by Lynn Reiser
Greenwillow 1993 (28p)
Despite language barriers, Margaret and Margarita meet in the park and play together.
In English and Spanish.

It's My Birthday
by Helen Oxenbury
Candlewick 1994 (24p)
In this cumulative story, a child's animal friends bring him the ingredients for his birthday cake.

A Playhouse for Monster
by Virginia Mueller
Whitman 1985 (24p) Puffin 1988 paper
Little Monster is lonely in his playhouse until he shares it with a friend.

Yo! Yes?
by Chris Raschka
Orchard 1993 (32p)
Two boys meet on a street and decide to be friends.

Books for Teacher Read Aloud

Benjamin and Tulip
by Rosemary Wells
Dial 1977 pa (32p)
Tulip and Benjamin become friends after they stop fighting. **Available in Spanish as Lucas y Virginia.**

Don't Fidget a Feather
by Erica Silverman
Macmillan 1994 (32p)
Gander and Duck learn about friendship when a fox almost eats them.

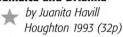

Ellen and Penguin
by Clara Vulliamy
Candlewick 1993 (32p)
Ellen and her favorite stuffed animal, Penguin, make friends with Jo and her stuffed monkey, Bill.

Frog and Toad Are Friends
by Arnold Lobel
Harper 1970 (64p) also paper
Five stories about Frog and Toad, two of the most beloved friends in children's literature. **Available in Spanish as Sapo y sepo son amigos.**

Jamaica and Brianna
by Juanita Havill
Houghton 1993 (32p)
Neither Jamaica nor her friend Brianna wants to wear hand-me-down boots.

Jessica
by Kevin Henkes
Greenwillow 1989 (24p) Puffin 1990 paper
Ruthie trades her imaginary friend Jessica for a real friend with the same name.

Best Friends for Frances
by Russell Hoban
Harper 1969 (32p) also paper
Frances the badger teaches her next-door neighbor Albert about friendship.

What's Claude Doing?
by Dick Gackenbach
Clarion 1984 (32p) paper
None of his animal friends can understand why Claude the dog won't come outside.

Jake and Rosie
by Patricia Lillie
Greenwillow 1989 (24p)
Jake is worried when his best friend, Rosie, is not at home.

Orson
by Rascal
Lothrop 1995 (24p)
Orson, a bear, has trouble making friends because he is so big.

Meg and Jack's New Friends
by Paul Dowling
Houghton 1990 (32p)
Sister and brother Meg and Jack, new in their neighborhood, experience different feelings about making friends.

We Are Best Friends
by Aliki
Greenwillow 1982 (32p) also paper
Robert and Peter are sad when Peter moves, but both make new friends.

Lost!
by David McPhail
Little, Brown 1990 (32p)
A boy becomes friends with a bear who is lost in the city. **Available in Spanish as *¡Perditos!***

William and Boomer
by Lindsay Barrett George
Greenwillow 1987 (24p)
William makes friends with a baby goose, and the two share a fun summer.

Books for Shared Reading

The Very Lonely Firefly
by Eric Carle
Philomel 1995 (32p)
A newly born firefly goes in search of other fireflies.

May I Bring a Friend?
by Beatrice Schenk de Regniers
Macmillan 1964 (32p) also paper
A boy invited to visit the king and queen brings along different animal friends every day of the week.

Fifty-five Friends
by Abbie Zabar
Hyperion 1994 (24p)
In an imaginary land, fifty-five unusual creatures are friends.

Carnival
 by Robin Ballard
Greenwillow 1995 (24p)
Didi looks forward to seeing her friend Emma dance in the carnival parade.

Copycat
by Ruth Brown
Dutton 1994 (32p)
Buddy, a cat, copies the actions of his three friends, two cats and a dog.

Do You See Mouse?
by Marion Crume
Silver 1995 (32p)
Five animal friends play hide-and-seek.

The Earth and I
 by Frank Asch
Gulliver 1994 (32)
A child explains his friendship with the earth.

Happy Birthday, Dear Duck
by Eve Bunting
Clarion 1988 (32p) also paper
Duck's birthday gifts don't seem to make sense—until the last gift is opened.

Let's Be Friends
by Caroline Ness
Harper 1994 (16p)
Two pets, a dog and a cat, learn how to be friends.

Mouse's Birthday
by Jane Yolen
Putnam 1993 (32p)
Mouse's friends don't fit into his small house so they help him find a bigger place.

Treasure Hunt
by Lorinda Bryan Cauley
Putnam 1994 (32p)
Children and their animal friends hunt for clues that lead them to a picnic lunch.

Technology Resources

Computer Resources

Internet See the Houghton Mifflin Internet resources for additional bibliographic entries and theme-related activities.

Video Cassettes

Frog and Toad Are Friends *by Arnold Lobel.* Pied Piper/AIMS Media

Frog and Toad Together *by Arnold Lobel.* Pied Piper/AIMS Media

I Have a Friend *by Keiko Narahashi.* SRA Media

Audio Cassettes

George and Martha *by James Marshall.* Houghton Mifflin

May I Bring a Friend? *by Beatrice Schenk de Regniers.* Weston Woods

Filmstrips

Let's Be Enemies *by Janice May Udry.* Weston Woods

Alexander and the Wind-Up Mouse *by Leo Lionni.* Am. Sch. Pub.

AV addresses are in the Teacher's Handbook, pages H14–H15.

Theme at a Glance

Reading/Listening Center

Selections	Comprehension Skills and Strategies	Phonemic Awareness	Phonics/Decoding	Concepts About Print
Jamaica's Find	✔ Drawing conclusions, T21 Using word and picture clues to draw conclusions, T28 What will happen next, T28 Guessing whose turn is next, T28 Reading strategies, T18, T22, T24 **Rereading and responding,** T26–T27	✔ Recognizing the first sound of a spoken word, T19 Sounds in animal names, T29 Matching first sounds, T29 Playing a matching game, T29		
What Shall We Do When We All Go Out?	✔ Sequence, T45 Story sequence, T56 Using words that tell when, T56 Sequence picture puzzles, T56 Reading strategies, T38, T40, T44, T46, T48, T50, T52 **Rereading and responding,** T54–T55		✔ Initial *f*, T47 Reading *f* words, T57 Things that begin with *f*, T57 Hide-and-seek *f*, T57 Recognizing *f* words, T58 Beginning sound riddles, T58 Beginning sound game, T58	✔ Left to right directionality, T41 Reading left to right, T59 Recognizing word order in a sentence, T59 Reading along with the audio tape, T59
Together	✔ Noting details, T75 Noting details about characters' actions, T86 Identifying characters' feelings, T86 Sharing work with a friend, T86 Noting details about setting, T86 Reading strategies, T70, T72, T76, T78, T82 **Rereading and responding,** T84–T85		✔ Initial *p*, T73 ✔ Phonogram *-ig*, T79 Reading *p* words, T87 Finding *p* words, T87 Collage of *p* words, T87 Spelling words with *-ig*, T88 Reading *-ig* words, T88 Practice with *-ig*, T88	✔ Beginning of a sentence, T81 Recognizing sentence beginnings, T89 Identifying and tallying sentences, T89 Reading directions, T89

✔ *Indicates Tested Skills. See page T11 for assessment options.*

Theme Concept

It's fun to be with, to share with, and to make new friends.

Pacing

This theme is designed to take $2\frac{1}{2}$ to 3 weeks, depending on your students' needs and interests.

Multi-Age Classroom

This theme can be used in conjunction with a theme found in another grade level.
Grade 1: Sharing Time

Writing/Language Center   Cross-Curricular Center

Vocabulary	Listening	Oral Language	Writing	Content Areas
		Making a telephone call, T30 Introducing oneself, T30 Describing words, T30 Opposites, T30	Lost and found posters, T31 Thank-you note, T31 Invitations, T31	**Social Studies:** friends in community, T32; making a map, T33 **Math:** graph of playground favorites, T32 **Music/Movement:** putting on a park show, T33
✓ High-frequency words: *in*, T51 Creating sentences with *in*, T60 Using a word in a sentence, T60 Word memory, T60	Finger rhyme, T61 Playing Simon Says, T61 Read along tape, T61	Role-playing, T62 Word web of school activities, T62 Welcoming a new child, T62	Class story, T37 Autograph book, T63 Friendship bulletin board, T63 Planning the day, T63	**Music/Movement:** singing and playing Follow the Leader, T64 **Art:** making a picture collage, T64 **Social Studies:** keeping play areas safe and clean, T65 **Science:** creating a seesaw, T65
✓ High-frequency words: *put*, T77 Playing the Hokey Pokey, T90 Working together, T90 Reading high-frequency words, T90	Real and imaginary tasks, T91 Listening for rhyming words, T91 Read along tape, T91	Things that go together, T94 How to be a good friend, T94 Playing together, T94	Class story, T69 Paper dolls, T93 Word banks, T93 Friendship card, T95 Doing it together, T95 Safety posters, T95	**Music:** making music with glasses of water, T96 **Math:** graphing favorite ice cream flavors, T96 **Art:** building a house, T97 **Science:** things that float, T97

Meeting Individual Needs

Key to Meeting Individual Needs

 Students Acquiring English

Activities and notes throughout the lesson plans offer strategies to help children understand the selections and lessons.

 Challenge

Challenge activities and notes throughout the lesson plans suggest additional activities to stimulate critical and creative thinking.

 Extra Support

Activities and notes throughout the lesson plans offer additional strategies to help children experience success.

Managing Instruction

Flexible Groups and Independent Work

Simplify classroom management of small flexible groups by preparing well in advance. A minimum of two weeks is usually needed to show students expected behavior for independent work at centers or for self-selected reading. Once students are comfortable in the routines for independent work, begin working with small flexible groups for very short time frames; a focused, well-paced lesson of ten minutes is often a good starting point.

For further information on this and other Managing Instruction topics, see the *Professional Development Handbook.*

Performance Standards

During this theme, children will

- *recognize that family and friends help one another and share together*
- *retell or summarize and evaluate each selection*
- *apply comprehension skills: Draw Conclusions, Sequence, Noting Details*
- *recognize the first sound in a spoken word and identify words beginning with the sounds for g and p*
- *recognize words with the phonogram -ig*
- *recognize the high-frequency words in and put*
- *apply left-to-right directionality*
- *write a story*

Students Acquiring English	Challenge	Extra Support
Develop Key Concepts Children focus on Key Concepts through a finger rhyme, sound riddles, and creating graphs.	**Apply Critical Thinking** Children apply critical thinking by drawing conclusions, sequencing, and noting details by using clues in the words and the pictures.	**Receive Increased Instructional Time** Practice activities in the Reading/Listening Center provide support with noting important details, drawing conclusions, and following sequence. Children also work on the phonogram *-ig* and initial *p* and *f* sounds.
Expand Vocabulary Children use context and picture clues, discuss meanings, and model definitions. Children expand their vocabulary to include contractions, words that have opposite meanings, and rhyming words.	**Explore Topics of Interest** Activities that motivate further exploration include making a map, studying fish habitats, and meeting helpful workers in the community.	
Act as a Resource Children are asked to share different kinds of food they eat for lunch, dinner rituals, and things they do when they go out to play.	**Engage in Creative Thinking** Opportunities for creative expression include creating a seesaw, making music, and illustrating sentences.	**Provide Independent Reading** Children choose to explore books and to read independently when exciting, theme-related literature is made available (see Bibliography, T6–T7).

Additional Resources

Invitaciones

Develop bi-literacy with this integrated reading/language arts program in Spanish. Provides authentic literature and real-world resources from Spanish-speaking cultures.

Language Support

Translations of Big Books in Chinese, Hmong, Khmer, and Vietnamese.
Teacher's Booklet provides instructional support in English.

Students Acquiring English Handbook

Guidelines, strategies, and additional instruction for students acquiring English.

Planning for Assessment

Informal Assessment

Informal Assessment Checklist

- Reading and Responding

Observation Checklists

- Concepts About Print/Book Handling
- Responding to Literature and Decoding Behaviors and Strategies
- Writing Behaviors and Stages of Temporary Spelling
- Listening and Speaking Behaviors
- Story Retelling and Rereading

Literacy Activity Book

Recommended pages for students' portfolios:

- Recognize the First Sound in a Spoken Word, p. 105
- Personal Response, p. 106
- Comprehension: Sequence, p. 108
- Language Patterns, p. 112
- Phonics: Initial *p,* p. 114
- Phonics: Phonogram *-ig,* p. 115

Retellings–Oral/Written

- *Teacher's Assessment Handbook*

Formal Assessment

Kindergarten Literacy Survey

Evaluates children's literacy development. Provides holistic indicator of children's ability with

- Shared Reading/ Constructing Meaning
- Concepts About Print
- Phonemic Awareness
- Emergent Writing

Theme Skills Test

- Inferences: Drawing Conclusions
- Letter Sounds *f* and *p*
- Phonogram *-ig*
- High-Frequency Words: *in* and *put*

Portfolio Assessment

The portfolio icon signals portfolio opportunities throughout the theme.

Additional Portfolio Tips:

- Using Portfolios to Communicate with Parents During Conferences, T99

Launching the Theme

See the Houghton Mifflin **Internet** resources for additional activities.

Song Tape for Let's Be Friends: *"Make New Friends"*

INTERACTIVE LEARNING

Warm-up/Build Background

Singing the Theme Song

- Play the Song Tape, inviting children who know "Make New Friends" to sing along. (See lyrics in the Teacher's Handbook, page H10.)

- Ask children to share what they know about silver and gold. Guide them in seeing that silver and gold are both very beautiful but different, just as friends are.

- Then play the song again, asking children to sing along.

Interactive Bulletin Board

Friends are...

A friend is **someone to eat lunch with.**

A friend is **someone to play ball with.**

A friend is **someone to laugh with.**

A friend is **someone to share toys with.**

Friends Are... Invite children to share their ideas about what makes a friend. Children might:

- Draw pictures of friends sharing and doing things together.

- Find pictures in magazines of friends and friendly acts to include on the bulletin board.

- Brainstorm ways to complete the sentence "A friend is _____" and add them to the bulletin board.

Ongoing Project

Make a Fold-Out Book About Friends

Tell children that they will work together to create a class fold-out book about what they like to do with a friend. You might title the books, *Friends at Home and at School*. To organize the project you may wish to follow these steps:

- Have children brainstorm a list of things they like to do with a friend. Add to the list throughout the theme.

- Have children illustrate a page with something they like to do with a friend. Children may wish to choose from the ideas on the class list.

- Invite children to write, or dictate, a sentence for their drawings.

See the *Home/Community Connections Booklet* for theme-related materials.

Portfolio Opportunity

The Portfolio Opportunity icon highlights portfolio opportunities throughout the theme.

Choices for Centers

Creating Centers

Use these activities to create learning centers in the classroom.

Reading/Listening Center

- Look What I Found at the Park, T29
- From Start to Finish, T58
- You'll Cut and I'll Paste, T87

Language/Writing Center

- Lost and Found Posters, T31
- Autograph Book, T63
- Friendship Card, T95

Cross-Curricular Center

- Playground Favorites, T32
- Creating a Seesaw, T65
- Making Music, T96

READ ALOUD

SELECTION:

Jamaica's Find

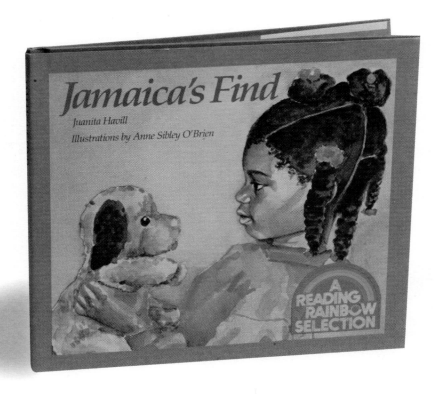

by Juanita Havill
illustrated by
Anne Sibley O'Brien

Other Books by Juanita Havill

Jamaica Tag-Along

Sato and the Elephants

Treasure Nap

- IRA/CBC Children's Choices
- Reading Rainbow Book
- Child Study Children's Book Award
- Best Books for Children
- Library of Congress Children's Books of the Year

Selection Summary

Jamaica finds a hat and a stuffed dog at the playground. She turns in the hat to the Lost and Found but decides to take the dog home. That night, with the help of her mother, Jamaica discovers her conscience and decides to turn in the lost dog. The new friend she makes by doing so proves an even bigger find!

Lesson Planning Guide

	Skill/Strategy Instruction	Meeting Individual Needs	Lesson Resources
1 **Introduce** *the* **Literature** *Pacing: 1 day*	**Preparing to Listen and Write** Warm-up/Build Background, T16 Read Aloud, T16	Choices for Rereading, T17	**Poster** Oh Where, Oh Where Has My Little Dog Gone? T16 *Literacy Activity Book* Personal Response, p. 103 **Song Tape** for Let's Be Friends: "Oh Where, Oh Where Has My Little Dog Gone?"
2 **Interact** *with* **Literature** *Pacing: 1-2 days*	**Reading Strategies** Monitor, T18 Self-Question, T18 Evaluate, T22 Summarize, T24 **Minilessons** ✓ Recognizing the First Sound of a Spoken Word, T19 ✓ Drawing Conclusions, T21	**Extra Support**, T19, T20, T26 **Students Acquiring English**, T21, T26, T27 **Challenge**, T26 **Rereading and Responding**, T26–T27	See the Houghton Mifflin **Internet** resources for additional activities.
3 **Instruct** *and* **Integrate** *Pacing: 1-2 days*	**Reading/Listening Center,** Comprehension, T28 Phonemic Awareness, T29 **Language/Writing Center,** Oral Language, T30 Writing, T31 **Cross-Curricular Center,** Cross-Curricular Activities, T32–T33	**Challenge**, T28, T33 **Extra Support**, T28, T29 **Students Acquiring English**, T30	**Poster** Community Friends, T32 **Letter, Word, and Picture Cards,** T29 *Literacy Activity Book* Comprehension, p. 104 Phonemic Awareness, p. 105 See the Houghton Mifflin **Internet** resources for additional activities.

✓ *Indicates **Tested Skills**. See page T11 for assessment options.*

1

Introduce
the
Literature

Preparing to Listen and Write

Poster

OH WHERE, OH WHERE
HAS MY LITTLE DOG GONE?

Oh where, oh where has my little dog gone?
Oh where, oh where can he be?
With his ears cut short and his tail cut long,
Oh where, oh where can he be?

Song Tape for Let's Be Friends:
*"Oh Where, Oh Where Has My Little
Dog Gone?"*

Literacy Activity Book, p. 103

I N T E R A C T I V E   L E A R N I N G

Warm-up/Build Background

Sharing a Song
- Invite children to follow along as you read the Poster "Oh Where, Oh Where Has My Little Dog Gone?"

- Play the song for children. (See lyrics and music in Teacher's Handbook, page H11.)

- Encourage them to tell how they feel when they lose something they like and when they find something someone else has lost. Discuss what a friend would do if he or she found something that belonged to someone else.

- Then play the song again, encouraging them to sing along.

Read Aloud
LAB, p. 103

Preview and Predict
- Display *Jamaica's Find*. Point out and read the title and the names of the author and the illustrator.

- Discuss the cover, leading children to identify what Jamaica is holding as a stuffed dog. See if children can relate the stuffed dog to the title.

- Preview pages 5-11 with children. Guide children in realizing that this is a realistic story; it tells about characters and things that could happen in real life. Ask them to predict what Jamaica might do with the dog.

Read
Read the story, pausing occasionally for children to comment on the illustrations and to predict what will happen next. Make sure children's predictions reflect an understanding of the story's realistic nature.

Personal Response
Home Connection Have children talk about the things Jamaica found. Then have children complete *Literacy Activity Book* page 103 to show something they have found. Invite children to take the page home and retell the story to their families.

Recognizing Problems and Solutions

To help children develop an understanding of the problems and solutions in the story, pause as you read to ask these questions:

- Page 21: What is Jamaica's problem?
  (She knows she should return the dog, but doesn't really want to.)

- Page 24: How does Jamaica solve her problem?
  (She finally decides to take the dog to the Lost and Found.)

- Page 29: What is Kristin's problem?
  (She has lost her stuffed animal, Edgar dog.)

- Page 31: How does Kristin solve her problem?
  (Jamaica takes Kristin to the Lost and Found, where she took Edgar dog.)

More Choices for Rereading

Rereadings provide varied, repeated experiences with the literature so that children can make its language and content their own. The following rereading choices appear on page T26.

- Pantomiming Story Scenes
- Sequence of Events
- Retelling *Jamaica's Find*
- A Different Point of View

Listening for Describing Words

As you read the story, have children raise their hands when they hear a word that describes another word. Prompt children as needed by asking questions such as:

- What words describe the hat Jamaica found? *(red, sock)*

- What words describe the dog Jamaica found? *(stuffed, cuddly, gray)*

- How does Jamaica's brother describe the dog? *(silly)*

List children's suggestions on chart paper. Retain the chart for later use.

Characters' Feelings

Help children identify story characters' feelings. Pause after reading pages 8, 17, 21, 24, 31, and 32 for them to tell how Jamaica feels. Encourage children to use text and picture clues and their own experiences to share their ideas.

Interact *with* Literature

READ ALOUD

Reading Strategies

▶ **Monitor**
Self-Question

Teacher Modeling Tell children that good listeners and readers do many things to help them enjoy and understand a story: they think about the important parts of the story so they can remember it; and they ask themselves questions about the things that happen. Model this with a Think Aloud.

Think Aloud

In this story, a girl named Jamaica finds a stuffed dog at the park. When Jamaica finds the dog, she puts it in her bicycle basket instead of taking it to the park house. When I ask myself why Jamaica did this, I think about what I might do. If I found a dog like that, I think I'd want to keep it. I think Jamaica wants to keep the dog, too.

Purpose Setting

As you read, invite children to think about what they would do if the things in the story happened to them. Allow time for children to express their feelings.

When Jamaica arrived at the park, there was no one there. It was almost supper time, but she still had a few minutes to play.

5

She sat in a swing, pushed off with her toes, and began pumping. It was fun not to have to watch out for the little ones who always ran in front of the swings.

7

QuickREFERENCE

Social Studies Link

If children notice that Jamaica isn't wearing a bike helmet, note that the story was written before bike laws were passed. Take this opportunity to discuss the importance of, and local laws regarding, bike helmets and bike safety.

Vocabulary

To help children understand the word *pumping* on page 7, ask how they swing in a swing. Note that they "pump" the swing by swinging their legs back and forth. Children might demonstrate pumping, using a chair as a swing.

Then she climbed up the slide. There was a red sock hat on the ladder step. Jamaica took it for a ride. She slid down so fast that she fell in the sand and lay flat on her back.

When she rolled over to get up, she saw a stuffed dog beside her. It was a cuddly gray dog, worn from hugging. All over it were faded food and grass stains. Its button nose must have fallen off. There was a round white spot in its place. Two black ears hung from its head.

8

Jamaica put the dog in her bicycle basket.

11

Read Aloud pp. 8–11

Phonemic Awareness

Recognizes the First Sound of a Spoken Word

TESTED SKILL

Teach/Model

Ask children to tell what Jamaica found at the park. (hat, dog) Ask children to listen for the beginning sound as you say *hat*.

Think Aloud

When I say the word *hat*, I hear /h/ at the beginning, the sound for *h*. I hear the /at/ sounds last, at the end of *hat*. What is the first sound you hear when I say *hat*—/h/ or /at/?

Follow a similar procedure, with the word *dog* and the sounds /d/ and /og/.

Practice/Apply

Have children say these words, listening for the beginning sound. Then ask them which sound they hear first in each word:

- park: /ark/ or /p/?
- red: /r/ or /ed/?
- sock: /s/ or /ock/?
- nose: /ose/ or /n/?

SKILL FINDER Sounds in Animal Names, page T29

Phonemic Awareness Review

Recognizes Alliteratives Ask children to listen as you reread the sentence on page 11. Ask them to listen for two words that begin with the same sound. (*bicycle, basket*)

MEETING INDIVIDUAL NEEDS
Extra Support

Phrase Meaning Discuss *worn with hugging,* comparing it to the more familiar *worn out*. Recall the poem "My Teddy Bear" from Theme 6. Ask if children have a stuffed animal that is *worn out* from being hugged or played with too much.

Multicultural Link

Explain to children that in many countries bicycles are an important means of transportation for people of all ages.

Interact
with
Literature

READ ALOUD

She took the hat into the park house and gave it to the young man at the counter.

12

The first thing her mother said when Jamaica came in the door was: "Where did that dog come from?"

"The park. I stopped to play on the way home," Jamaica said. "I found someone's red hat and took it to the Lost and Found."

"But, Jamaica, you should have returned the dog, too," said her mother. Then she said, "I'm glad you returned the hat."

"It didn't fit me," Jamaica said.

"Maybe the dog doesn't fit you either," her mother said.

"I like the dog," said Jamaica.

15

QuickREFERENCE

"Don't put that silly dog on the table!" Jamaica's brother said. "You don't know where it came from. It isn't very clean, you know," her father said.

16

"Not in the kitchen, Jamaica," her mother said. Jamaica took the dog to her room. She could hear her mother say, "It probably belongs to a girl just like Jamaica."

After dessert Jamaica went to her room very quietly. She held the dog up and looked at it closely. Then she tossed it on a chair.

18

Visual Literacy

Point out Jamaica's family on pages 16-17. Note that each family member does something to get ready for dinner: Jamaica's brother sets the table; her mother and father put food on the table. Ask children to talk about jobs they have at home.

Students Acquiring English

Ask children if they like dessert. Invite children to name and discuss some of their favorite desserts.

Comprehension
Drawing Conclusions

Teach/Model

Ask children to tell which item they would rather receive as a gift:

- A shirt or a video game?
- A belt or a paint set?
- A hat or a stuffed animal?

Use their responses to model for children how they can figure out why Jamaica returns the hat, but keeps the stuffed dog.

> **Think Aloud**
>
> I know that boys and girls usually like toys—rather than clothes—as gifts. I guess they think toys are more fun. This helps me see why Jamaica wants to keep the dog. It's a toy, it's lovable, and it's cute even though it's worn out from hugging.

Ask children to tell why Jamaica turned the hat into the Lost and Found. Why didn't she keep it?

Practice/Apply

Reread pages 15-23. Ask children to tell why Jamaica decided to return the dog. (Her family helps her realize that keeping the dog wouldn't be fair to the rightful owner.)

SKILL FINDER

Drawing Conclusions, page T28

Minilessons, Themes 2, 5, 12

Interact *with* Literature

READ ALOUD

Reading Strategies

▶ **Evaluate**

Teacher Modeling Explain that good listeners and readers think about the story characters and ask themselves if they agree with what the characters do. This helps them decide whether or not they like a story.

Think Aloud

At first, I thought I'd like to keep the dog, just like Jamaica did. But after reading the things her mother says, Jamaica began thinking about the dog's real owner. This made me think about the dog's real owner, too. It made me think that maybe I was wrong to want to keep the dog.

Ask if children, too, have changed their minds about whether or not Jamaica should keep the dog.

"Jamaica," her mother called from the kitchen. "Have you forgotten? It's your turn to dry the dishes."

"Do I have to, Mother? I don't feel good," Jamaica answered. Jamaica heard the pots rattle. Then she heard her mother's steps.

21

Her mother came in quietly, sat down by Jamaica, and looked at the stuffed dog, which lay alone on the chair. She didn't say anything. After a while she put her arms around Jamaica and squeezed for a long time.

"Mother, I want to take the dog back to the park," Jamaica said.

"We'll go first thing in the morning." Her mother smiled.

23

Jamaica ran to the park house and plopped the stuffed dog on the counter.

"I found this by the slide," she told the young man.

"Oh, hi. Aren't you the girl who gave me the hat last night?"

"Yes," said Jamaica, feeling hot around her ears.

"You sure do find a lot of things. I'll put it on the Lost and Found shelf." Jamaica stood watching him.

"Is that all?" he asked. "You didn't find anything else, did you?"

"No. That's all." She stayed to watch him put the dog on a shelf behind him.

"I'm sure some little girl or boy will come in after it today, a nice little dog like that," the young man said.

24

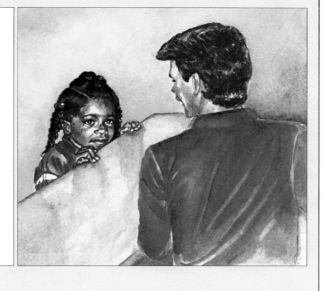

Jamaica ran outside. She didn't feel like playing alone. There was no one else at the park but her mother, who sat on a bench. Then Jamaica saw a girl and her mother cross the street to the park.

"Hi. I'm Jamaica. What's your name?" she said to the girl.

26

The girl let go of her mother's hand. "Kristin," she said.

"Do you want to climb the jungle gym with me, Kristin?" Jamaica said.

27

Science Link

Encourage children to discuss the picture on pages 26-27. Ask if they can tell what time of year the story takes place. (Fall/autumn: The leaves are changing color on the trees; the characters are wearing long-sleeved shirts and sweaters.)

2

Interact with Literature

READ ALOUD

Kristin ran toward Jamaica. "Yes, but I have to find something first."

"What?" asked Jamaica. Kristin was bending under the slide.

"What did you lose?" said Jamaica.

"Edgar dog. I brought him with me yesterday and now I can't find him," Kristin answered.

"Was he kind of gray with black ears?" Jamaica couldn't keep from shouting. "Come along with me."

29

Reading Strategies

▶ **Summarize**

Teacher Modeling Help children summarize the story by telling what happens at the beginning, in the middle, and at the end. Display the story pages cited as you model your thinking:

Think Aloud

At the beginning of the story (pages 8–9), Jamaica finds a hat and a stuffed dog at the park. In the middle (pages 12–13), Jamaica returns the hat and keeps the dog; but she finally decides to return the dog too. The story ends (pages 30–32) when Jamaica helps Kristin get back her stuffed dog and makes a new friend.

Display the pages a spread at a time, inviting children to use the pictures as prompts to retell it in their own words.

The young man in the park house looked over the counter at the two girls.

"Now what have you found?" he asked Jamaica.

But this time Jamaica didn't drop anything onto the counter. Instead, she smiled her biggest smile. "I found the girl who belongs to that stuffed dog."

31

Self-Assessment

Have children ask themselves:

- Do I think about what happens at the beginning, in the middle, and at the end of a story when I want to retell it?
- When I listen to or read a story, do I think about whether I agree or disagree with things the characters do?
- Do I think about the way a story makes me feel?

Jamaica was almost as happy as Kristin, who took Edgar dog in her arms and gave him a big welcome-back hug.

32

Read Aloud p. 32

QuickREFERENCE

Social Studies Link

Identify the map on page 30 as a map of the park, and ask how people visiting the park might use it. Encourage children to name other places they have seen maps. (subway stations, post offices, department stores, road maps in family cars)

Visual Literacy

Note the badge on the man's pocket and the green shirt that he wears on both days. Help children conclude the man is wearing a uniform. Ask why park workers might wear uniforms. Have children name other people who wear uniforms.

Interact with Literature

Rereading

Choices for Rereading

Pantomiming Story Scenes

Invite children to retell their favorite scenes in the story. Then read the entire story, inviting children to take turns pantomiming the various scenes as you read.

Sequence of Events

Extra Support As you read the story, stop now and then for children to identify the sequence of events. Prompt children as needed by asking questions such as:

- What happened *first?*
- What happened *next?*
- What happened *last?*

Students Acquiring English This framework is a good way to help children acquiring English summarize story events.

Retelling *Jamaica's Find*

Provide children with a stuffed dog and red hat, similar to the ones Jamaica found. Invite them to use these props to dramatize the story.

Materials
- small stuffed dog
- red knit hat

A Different Point of View

Challenge Invite children to tell the story from a different point of view—that of Edgar dog. As you read the story, stop after each spread for children to create dialogue for the dog. Encourage them to tell what Edgar dog might say to Jamaica if he could talk.

Informal Assessment

Use Story Talk or the dramatization activity to assess children's general understanding of *Jamaica's Find*. Also note children's ability to recognize that print is read from top to bottom.

Responding

Choices for Responding

Story Talk

Place children in groups of three or four to talk about the story. Children might discuss:

- why Jamaica wanted to keep the dog at first
- why Jamaica changed her mind about keeping the dog
- how Kristin must have felt when Edgar dog was lost
- what they would do if they found a dog or other toy in a park

A Time I Changed My Mind

Note that Jamaica decides to keep the dog but later changes her mind and returns it. Ask children to think about a time they wanted something but later changed their minds about it. Have children draw a picture of the thing they wanted. As children share their drawings, encourage them to tell why they changed their minds about wanting the item.

Creating New Scenes

Have children work in groups to act out other endings, such as what may have happened if Jamaica didn't return the dog and met Kristin in the park, or what may have happened if the dog Jamaica found wasn't Kristin's after all.

Students Acquiring English Placing children acquiring English in mixed language groupings for this activity will help them gain proficiency.

Finders Keepers

Recite for children the familiar saying "Finders keepers, losers weepers." Talk about the meaning of the rhyme. Ask children how the story might have been different if Jamaica believed this. Invite children to tell whether or not they think the idea of "Finders keepers" is fair.

Portfolio Opportunity

For a writing sample, save children's responses to A Time I Changed My Mind.

Instruct
and
Integrate

Comprehension

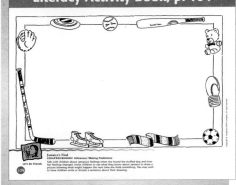

Literacy Activity Book, p. 104

Practice Activities

Drawing Conclusions

LAB, p. 104

Extra Support Display *Jamaica's Find*, and recall what the story is about. Remind children that we can use word and picture clues to figure out things in a story. Then invite children to use word and picture clues to answer these questions:

pages 12-13   Why does Jamaica take the hat to the park house? (It is where people take "found" things.)

pages 22-23   Why does Jamaica's mother smile? (She is proud Jamaica made the decision to return the dog.)

pages 30-31   Why does the man ask, "Now what have you found?" (Jamaica has found two things; he thinks she has found something else.)

Have children complete *Literacy Activity Book* page 104.

What Next?

Ask children what they think Kristin and Jamaica will do now that Kristin has her stuffed dog back. Reread pages 26-29, asking children to listen for clues that will help them tell what Kristin and Jamaica will do. Have them draw and write about their ideas.

Invite small groups of children to discuss what other things Kristin and Jamaica might do together at the park. Have groups share their ideas with the class.

Who's Turn?

Revisit pages 16-21 to help children conclude that everyone in Jamaica's family helps at dinner time. Have children use word and picture clues to tell what each family member does. (brother, set the table; mother and father, get dinner ready; Jamaica, dry the dishes; mother, wash the dishes)

Challenge Ask children what might happen if Jamaica and her brother take turns doing dinner-time chores. What will Jamaica's job be at dinner next time? (to set the table) What will her brother's job be? (to dry the dishes)

Informal Assessment

As children complete the activities, note their ability to draw conclusions and recognize the first sound of a spoken word.

Phonemic Awareness

Practice Activities

Literacy Activity Book, p. 105

Sounds in Animal Names

LAB, p. 105

Extra Support Ask children to tell what kind of stuffed animal Jamaica found at the park. (dog) Ask children to listen as you say *dog*. Ask what sound they hear first in the word–/d/ or /og/. (/d/) Repeat the procedure with the names for other stuffed animals she might have found:

- bear: /b/ or /ear/?
- horse: /h/ or /orse/?
- duck: /uck/ or /d/?
- mouse: /ouse/ or /m/?
- goat: /g/ or /oat/?
- seal: /eal/ or /s/?

Have children complete *Literacy Activity Book* page 105.

Matching First Sounds

Ask children to listen carefully as you say a word. Say *red*. Ask which word–*bed* or *ring*–has the same first sound as *red*. (ring) Repeat the procedure with the following words and word pairs.

- coat: *goat* or *cow?*
- house: *mouse* or *ham?*
- jar: *jump* or *car?*
- king: *kite* or *wing?*
- box: *ball* or *fox?*
- top: *mop* or *tooth?*

Look What I Found at the Park

- Have children sit in a circle; then pass out the Picture Cards.

- Tell children to pass the cards around the circle. When you ring the bell, they are to stop passing the cards.

- Ask children to listen as you say a word, for example, *bear*.

- If the word has the same first sound as the name of the picture they are holding, children hold up the card(s) and say, "Look what I found at the park." Remove the card(s) from play.

- Continue until all Picture Cards are collected.

Materials

- Picture Cards: *ball, balloon, bat, bike, cane, camera, doll, feather, game, ghost, horn, jacket, kite, keys, marbles, mask, mittens, necklace, pencil, radio, ring, top, wagon, yo-yo*
- bell

Portfolio Opportunity

- For a record of children's understanding of beginning sounds, save *Literacy Activity Book* page 105.

- Save the activity What Next? as a record of children's ability to draw conclusions.

Instruct *and* **Integrate**

Oral Language

Choices for Oral Language

Making a Telephone Call

Encourage children to role-play making a telephone call to respond to one of the Lost and Found posters their classmates made (see page T31). Make sure children identify themselves, tell why they are calling, and ask to speak to the person who placed the ad.

Introducing Oneself

Recall how Jamaica introduced herself to Kristin, asked her name, and invited her to play. Invite children to practice introducing themselves to others. Have pairs of children role play making introductions and asking their new friends to play.

Describing Words

Display the list of adjectives children generated while completing Listening for Describing Words, page T17. Read through the list with children. Help them organize the words and encourage them to suggest others to add to the web.

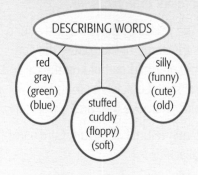

DESCRIBING WORDS

red
gray
(green)
(blue)

stuffed
cuddly
(floppy)
(soft)

silly
(funny)
(cute)
(old)

Lost and Found

 Students Acquiring English Talk about the words *lost* and *found*, noting that the words have opposite meanings. Ask children to suggest opposites for the following:

go (stop) off (on) soft (hard)
hot (cold) over (under) long (short)
in (out) big (small) fast (slow)

Invite children to choose an opposite pair to illustrate. Have them draw two pictures that show the meaning of each word. Invite children to label their drawings if they wish.

Informal Assessment

- Use the activities on this page to track children's oral language development.
- As children complete the writing activities, note their use of correct directional patterns.

 # Writing

Choices for Writing

Lost and Found Posters

Discuss lost and found notices with children. Then invite children to make their own Lost and Found posters. Children should:

- think about something they have recently lost or found,
- draw a picture of the item,
- label their drawings with the words Lost or Found,
- give other information that might help tell about the item,
- include their name and phone number on the posters.

> **LOST**
> in the library
> 1 red mitten
> Please call David
> at 277-4215

Thank You, Jamaica

Suggest to children that Kristin might write a thank-you note to Jamaica for finding Edgar dog. Ask children to fold a piece of drawing paper in half to create a card. Invite them to write the words *Thank You* on the cover. Encourage them to write a special message to Jamaica on the inside.

Come and Play

Recall with children that Jamaica invited Kristin to play. Mention that one way we invite people to do things is to send an invitation. Guide children in designing an invitation frame that they can complete to invite a friend to come and play.

 Portfolio Opportunity

Any one of the activities on this page might be saved as a record of children's written work.

3

Instruct *and* Integrate

Cross-Curricular Activities

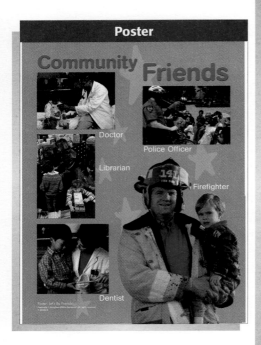

Poster

Community Friends

Doctor

Police Officer

Librarian

Firefighter

Dentist

Social Studies

Friends in Our Community

Recall with children the man at the park house who helped Jamaica. Explain that many workers in a community are our friends and are there to help us. Display the poster "Community Friends." Encourage children to name the workers pictured and tell how these people are our friends.

If your community has a Neighborhood Watch, Safe Haven, or Helping Hand program, mention it at this time. Display the symbol or sign associated with the program for children to talk about. Mention that if children are lost or need any help in any way, the homes or shops displaying this symbol can help them.

Challenge Ask children to draw and write about a community worker who has helped them in some way. Invite them to share their drawings with the class.

Math

Playground Favorites

Recall with children the playground equipment at Jamaica's park. *(swings, slide, jungle gym)* Encourage children to name other things they might play on at a park, such as a seesaw or a round-about. Then ask each child to tell the one thing he or she likes most. Make a bar graph to record their responses.

How Many?	1	2	3	4	5	6	7
Swings							
Slide							
Jungle Gym							
Seesaw							
Round-About							

Social Studies

Making a Map

MEETING INDIVIDUAL NEEDS

Challenge Recall with children the map on the park house wall. Discuss with children how such a map might be used. Help children understand the function of a map by displaying a simple picture map. Prompt children to locate items on the map by asking questions.

Then invite children to help you create a map of the school and the surrounding streets. You may wish to take children on a walk around the grounds to note street signs, buildings, playgrounds, parks, and other features before making the map.

To make the map, sketch in the school building and the surrounding streets for children. Children can then add in the other features they noted. Help children label the map as needed.

Materials
- butcher block paper
- crayons or markers
- a simple picture map from a math or social studies text

Music/Movement

Putting on a Park Show

Mention to children that many parks have special shows during the week or on the weekends for people to enjoy. Brainstorm with children a list of some of the things they may see:

singers	mimes	musicians
dancers	actors	acrobats

Invite children to work in small groups to choose one kind of entertainer on the list. Then suggest they prepare a show to put on for the class.

Materials
- classroom instruments
- cassette player
- assorted items child might need

BIG BOOK

SELECTION:

What Shall We Do When We All Go Out?

Big Book

Little Big Book

illustrated by Shari Halpern

Other Books by Shari Halpern

I Have a Pet!

My River

Moving from One to Ten

Selection Summary

The question posed in the traditional song "What Shall We Do When We All Go Out?" is answered by a brother and sister who, in between breakfast, lunch, and dinner, spend their day bike riding, seesawing, somersaulting, roller-skating, kite flying, tree climbing, and more.

Lesson Planning Guide

	Skill/Strategy Instruction	Meeting Individual Needs	Lesson Resources
1 **Introduce** *the* **Literature** *Pacing: 1 day*	**Shared Reading and Writing** Warm-up, T36 Shared Reading, T36 Shared Writing, T37	Choices for Rereading, T37	**Poster** With a Friend, T36 *Literacy Activity Book* Personal Response, p.106 **Audio Tape** for Let's Be Friends: *What Shall We Do When We All Go Out?*
2 **Interact** *with* **Literature** *Pacing: 1–2 days*	**Reading Strategies** Evaluate, T38, T48, T50 Self-Question, T40, T44 Monitor, T40, T44 Think About Words, T46 Summarize, T50 Monitor, T52 **Minilessons** ✓ Left to Right Directionality, T41 ✓ Sequence, T45 ✓ Initial *f*, T47 ✓ High-Frequency Words: *in*, T51	**Students Acquiring English,** T40, T44, T51, T52, T54 **Extra Support,** T38, T39, T41, T47 **Rereading and Responding,** T54-T55	**Letter, Word, and Picture Cards,** T47, T51, T55 **Story Retelling Props,** T55 *Literacy Activity Book* Language Patterns, p. 107 See the Houghton Mifflin **Internet** resources for additional activities.
3 **Instruct** *and* **Integrate** *Pacing: 1–2 days*	**Reading/Listening Center,** Comprehension, T56 Phonics/Decoding, T57–T58 Concepts About Print, T59 Vocabulary, T60 Listening, T61 **Language/Writing Center,** Oral Language, T62 Writing, T63 **Cross-Curricular Center,** Cross-Curricular Activities, T64–T65	**Extra Support,** T56, T57, T58, T59, T60, T63 **Challenge,** T58, T60, T62, T63, T65	**Poster** With a Friend, T59 **Letter, Word, and Picture Cards,** T57, T58, T59, T60 **My Big Dictionary,** T57 **Game:** Friendship Fun, T58, H6 *Literacy Activity Book* Comprehension, p. 108 Phonics/Decoding, p. 109 Vocabulary, p. 110 **Audio Tape** for Let's Be Friends: *What Shall We Do When We All Go Out?* See the Houghton Mifflin **Internet** resources for additional activities.

✓ *Indicates Tested Skills. See page T11 for assessment options.*

Introduce *the* Literature

Shared Reading and Writing

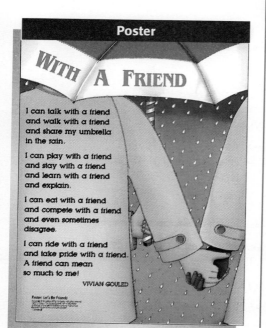

Poster

WITH A FRIEND

I can talk with a friend
and walk with a friend
and share my umbrella
in the rain.

I can play with a friend
and stay with a friend
and learn with a friend
and explain.

I can eat with a friend
and compete with a friend
and even sometimes
disagree.

I can ride with a friend
and take pride with a friend.
A friend can mean
so much to me!

VIVIAN GOULED

Audio Tape for Let's Be Friends: *What Shall We Do When We All Go Out?*

Literacy Activity Book, p. 106

INTERACTIVE LEARNING

Warm-up

Sharing Poetry
- Display the poster for "With a Friend" and read the title.
- Read the poem aloud as children follow along with the words.
- Ask children to read the poem along with you and to raise their hands when they say something that they like to do with a friend.

Shared Reading

LAB, p. 106

Preview and Predict
- Display *What Shall We Do When We All Go Out?* Point to and read aloud the title and the illustrator's name.
- Ask if children have ever sung a song with this same title. (You might wish to play the Audio Tape, inviting children to sing along.)
- Read aloud through page 7. If children sang the song, lead them to see that the words on these pages are the same. Encourage them to predict what the brother and sister will do when they go out to play.

Read Together
- Read the selection aloud, emphasizing the rhythm of the words. Encourage children to chime in on repeated phrases and on any other words they know.
- As you read, invite children to comment on the illustrations. Pause after pages 19 and 29 to note the change in the time of day. Encourage them to make predictions about what the children might do next.

Personal Response
Have children complete *Literacy Activity Book* page 106 to show which of the things the brother and sister did that they too would like to do.

Shared Writing: *A Class Story*

Brainstorming   Have children recall the things the children in the story did. Then invite children to write their own version of the story, for things they do in school. Have them brainstorm a list of school-related activities to include in the story.

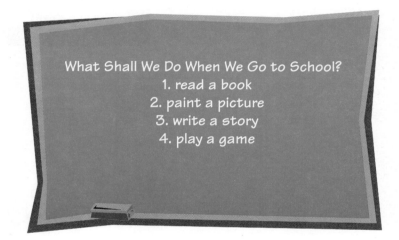

What Shall We Do When We Go to School?
1. read a book
2. paint a picture
3. write a story
4. play a game

Drafting   Record the first verse of the class story on chart paper, substituting the words *all go out* with *go to school.* Have children use their ideas to write a second verse and subsequent verses of the story. Offer assistance in keeping to the language pattern of the story.

Publishing   Have children illustrate the story verses. Then invite them to sing their story. Record their singing and place the tape along with the story in the Reading and Listening Center.

Choices for Rereading

Rereadings provide varied, repeated experiences with the literature so children can make its language and content their own. Choices for rereading appear on page T54.

- Exploring Language Patterns
- Cooperative Reading
- Singing the Song
- Acting Out the Song

Portfolio Opportunity

Save *Literacy Activity Book* page 106 as a record of children's response to the literature.

Interact *with* Literature

Reading Strategies

 Evaluate

Discussion Remind children that one thing good readers do when they read a story is think about whether the story tells about things that could really happen or if it is make-believe. Encourage children to tell what kind of story this is. Help children see that even though the art might look "make-believe" the brother and sister in the story behave like real brothers and sisters might.

Purpose Setting

As children reread the story, have them think about the different things the brother and sister do and when they do it.

BIG BOOK

What shall we do when we all go out, all go out, all go out?

4

High-Frequency Words

Call on volunteers to frame the word *go* on page 4. Ask children how many times the word appears on the page. (three)

MEETING INDIVIDUAL NEEDS **Extra Support**

Word Meaning Focus attention on the word *shall*. Explain that this is another way of saying *will*.

Visual Literacy

Ask children what the brother and sister are doing on pages 4-5 as they wonder what to do when they go out. (eating breakfast) Ask children if they, too, think about what they will do during the day as they eat breakfast.

What shall we do when we all go out,
When we all go out to play?

Extra Support

End Punctuation You might wish to point out the question mark at the end of the line on page 7. Mention to children that this mark shows the end of a sentence that asks a question.

2

Interact
with
Literature

BIG BOOK

We will ride our three-wheel bikes,
three-wheel bikes, three-wheel bikes.
We will ride our three-wheel bikes
When we all go out to play!

8

Reading Strategies

▶ **Self-Question/ Monitor**

Discussion Remind children that good readers ask themselves questions about the things that happen in the story. Ask children where they think the brother and sister went to play. (park or playground) Encourage children to tell how they know.

Quick REFERENCE

Vocabulary

Ask children if they know another word for a three-wheeled bike. (a tricycle) Encourage children to tell what kind of bikes they ride.

MEETING INDIVIDUAL NEEDS
Students Acquiring English

This is a good story for students acquiring English because the pictures provide clues and the pattern is easy to follow.

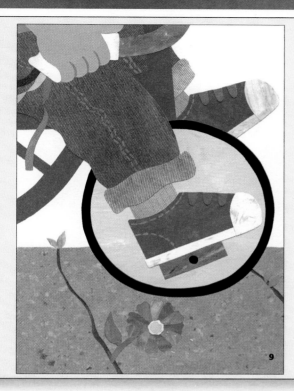

We will seesaw up and down,
up and down, up and down.
We will seesaw up and down
When we all go out to play!

9

MINILESSON

Concepts About Print

Left to Right Directionality

TESTED SKILL

Teach/Model

Ask children to watch carefully as you point to and read the first line on page 8. Read the line aloud, running your hands under the words in a sweeping motion.

Think Aloud

When we read, we read the words in a sentence in a certain order, from left to right. Watch as I read the first line again.

Reread the line, running your hands under the words.

Practice/Apply

Call on a volunteer to come to the front of the room and point to the words in the first line on page 8 as you read them aloud. When the child reaches the end of the line, thank him or her, and ask for another volunteer to point to the first word that should be read in the next line. Continue with all the lines on the page.

SKILL FINDER

Reading Left to Right, page T59

Minilessons, Themes 2, 6

Math Link

Ask children to name the shape that the seesaw board is on. (triangle) Have them tell how many sides a triangle has. (three) Ask how many triangles appear on the page. (three)

MEETING INDIVIDUAL NEEDS **Extra Support**

Word Meaning Ask if children have ever played on a *seesaw* before. Encourage those who have to tell how the seesaw goes up and down. Some children may know a seesaw by the name *teeter-totter*.

2 Interact *with* **Literature**

12

We will wear our roller skates,
roller skates, roller skates.
We will wear our roller skates
When we all go out to play!

14

QuickREFERENCE

Movement

Call on volunteers to demonstrate for the class how to somersault. You may wish to place a mat or blanket on the floor before children do their somersaults.

*We will run and somersault,
somersault, somersault.
We will run and somersault
When we all go out to play!*

13

15

Math Link

Have children count the number of skates they see on pages 14-15. (four) How many wheels are on each skate? (four) How many wheels do you see altogether? (sixteen)

Interact *with* Literature

BIG BOOK

*Then we'll sit and eat our lunch,
eat our lunch, eat our lunch.
Then we'll sit and eat our lunch
In the middle of the day!*

16

Reading Strategies

▶ **Self-Question/ Monitor**

Discussion Ask if children had any questions after reading pages 16-19. For example, some children may wonder where the picnic lunch came from. Help children use picture clues to conclude that the children probably had their lunches in their backpacks.

Ask if children see anything else in the backpacks that might help them predict what the children will do after lunch. (The tail of a kite is hanging from the girl's backpack; the children will fly kites.)

*What shall we do in the afternoon,
afternoon, afternoon?
What shall we do in the afternoon
After we've had lunch?*

QuickREFERENCE

Health/Nutrition Link

Invite children to tell what the brother and sister are eating for lunch. (sandwich, juice or milk) Then invite children to tell what they like to eat for lunch. Talk about the importance of eating a good lunch.

 Students Acquiring English

Invite children to talk about what they like to eat for lunch. In many countries lunch is the biggest meal of the day.

19

Comprehension

Sequence

Teach/Model

Tell children that often when they read, they will find words that help readers figure out when things happen in a story. Invite children to reread pages 16-19 with you. Use a Think Aloud to identify the words that tell when.

Think Aloud

On page 16, the word *then* tells me what the children do after they roller skate. The words *in the middle of the day* tell me when they ate lunch.

Read pages 18-19 to help children find words that help them figure out when things happen. (*In the afternoon* tells what time during the day; *after we've had lunch* tells when they feed the ducks.)

Practice/Apply

Reread pages 26-27. Ask: What words help tell how long the children will play hide-and-seek? (till it's time for us to go)

Reread pages 30-31. Ask: What word names a time that hasn't come yet? (tomorrow)

SKILL FINDER	Story Sequence, page T56
	Minilessons, Themes 1, 3, 8, and 11

Vocabulary

Ask children what time of day it is when it is *afternoon*. (after lunch time, but before dinner) Explain to children that afternoon begins after noon, or 12 o'clock. Encourage children to tell what they do after noon.

Social Studies Link

Ask children what the picture on page 19 shows. (the girl throwing away the trash from lunch) Note with children that this is a friendly thing to do not only for the environment but also for other people who will visit and want to enjoy the park or playground.

Interact *with* Literature

Reading Strategies

▶ **Think About Words**

Discuss how children could figure out the word *ducks* on page 20.

The story says: *We will stop to feed the ___, feed the ___, feed the ___.*

- **What makes sense** This word names something the children feed in the park. They might feed *birds, ducks, fish, squirrels,* or other animals.

- **Sounds for letters** What letter does the word begin with? *(d)* What word names something children can feed at a park and that begins with the sound for *d*?

- **Picture clues** The picture shows the children feeding a mother duck and her ducklings. The word must be *ducks*.

Have children read the sentence on page 20 with you. Ask if the word *ducks* makes sense.

We will stop to feed the ducks, feed the ducks, feed the ducks. We will stop to feed the ducks After we've had lunch!

20

We will fly our long-tailed kites, long-tailed kites, long-tailed kites. We will fly our long-tailed kites After we've had lunch!

22

Quick**REFERENCE**

Science Link

Ask if children know what a baby duck is called. *(duckling)* If children created charts to list the names of animals and their babies for *Animal Mothers* or for the *In the Barnyard* theme, you may wish to review these charts with children.

Big Book pp. 21, 23

Extra Support

Word Meaning Help children identify the *tail* of a kite. Then ask if they can name other things that have tails. (animals) Encourage children to tell how animal and kite tails are alike and different.

Phonics/Decoding

Initial *f*

TESTED SKILL

Teach/Model

Display pages 20-21. Ask children what the brother and sister will do after they've had lunch. (feed the ducks) Have children say *feed,* listening for the beginning sound. Then display Magic Picture *fish*.

Note that Magic Picture *fish* helps children remember the sound for *f*. Have children say *feed* and *fish*, listening for the beginning sound. Conclude that *feed* has the same beginning sound as *fish*.

Have volunteers find and frame the word *feed* four times on page 20. Note with children that the word *feed* begins with the letter *f*.

Practice/Apply

Read aloud the following words. Have children raise their hands when they hear a word that begins with the sound for *f*.

fun	play	follow
hands	feet	finger
four	five	six

SKILL FINDER ► Reading *F* Words, page T57

Interact *with* Literature

We will climb a great big tree,
a great big tree, a great big tree.
We will climb a great big tree
When we all go back to play!

Reading Strategies

▶ **Evaluate**

Discussion Have children think about the things the brother and sister have done in the story so far. Do they still think the children are acting like real brothers and sisters? Why or why not?

We will all play hide-and-seek,
hide-and seek, hide-and-seek.
We will all play hide-and-seek
till it's time for us to go!

26

QuickREFERENCE

Visual Literacy

Ask children how the artist helps show how big the tree is that the children climb. Note, if children do not, that only a small part of the tree is shown and yet it still fills the page; it must be a very big tree.

25

Big Book pp. 25, 27

Visual Literacy

Invite children to play hide-and-seek on pages 26-27, asking if they can find one of the children and the dog. (The hands are easily seen, but they may have to look for the dog's tail protruding from the side of the bush.)

Multicultural Link

Hide-and-seek is played round the world with many variations. Invite children to share versions they know such as sardines, hot-and-cold, or kick-the-can.

Interact
with
Literature

Reading Strategies

 Evaluate

Discussion Invite children to share their feelings about the story. You might prompt them with questions such as:

- Do you like the story? Why or why not?

- How do you feel about the art?

- Do you think it was a good idea for the author to turn a song into a story? Why or why not?

▶ **Summarize**

Discussion Recall that in *ABC and You*, the alphabet helped children remember the order of things in the story; in *Ten Black Dots*, numbers helped them.

Ask what helps children remember the order of events in this story. (breakfast, lunch, and dinner) Page through the story, asking children to use picture clues to tell the events that happen after breakfast, after lunch, and at dinner.

BIG BOOK

*What shall we do when we all go in,
all go in, all go in?
What shall we do when we all go in,
When we all go in from play?*

28

30

QuickREFERENCE

Phonemic Awareness Review

Alliteratives Read the first line on page 29. Ask if children notice that three of the words begin with the same sound. Have them say *sit*, *sip*, and *soup*. Then frame each word and have the initial letter named.

29

We will sit and sip our soup,
sip our soup, sip our soup.
We will sit and sip our soup
And think about TOMORROW!

Vocabulary

High-Frequency Words: *in*

TESTED ✓ SKILL

Teach/Model

Display Word Card *in*. Read the word aloud. Then ask:

- How many letters are in *in*?

- What letter does *in* begin with? End with?

Invite children to help you read page 28. Have them name the word that tells where the brother and sister will go. *(in)* Ask children to compare the word *in* in the text to the Word Card *in*, letter for letter.

Practice/Apply

Use Word and Picture Cards to create this sentence in a pocket chart:

I go in the .

Read the sentence with children, asking a volunteer to frame the word *in*. Then invite children to suggest other things they can go in. Replace Picture Card *house* with a Word or Picture Card to represent their ideas. Invite them to read their new sentences.

SKILL FINDER — Creating Sentences with *In*, page T60

QuickREFERENCE

Ask children what time they eat dinner in their house. What types of food do they eat? If children have a certain meal on the same night each week, invite them to discuss their ritual.

Interact *with* Literature

Reading Strategies

▶ **Monitor**

Discussion Invite children to talk about the last page of the story. Ask how they can use this page to help them decide what the brother and sister do after dinner.

Self-Assessment

Have children ask themselves:
● Am I able to use picture clues to retell the story? Can I think about the order in which the events happened?

QuickREFERENCE

Students Acquiring English

A natural extension for this story is to ask children from different cultural backgrounds to talk about what they typically do when they go out to play.

2

Interact
with
Literature

Rereading

Literacy Activity Book, p. 107

We will _____
When we all go out to play!

What Shall We Do When We All Go Out?
LANGUAGE PATTERNS
Children draw something that they have fun doing with a friend. Then they write or dictate the name of the activity to complete the language pattern from the selection.
Let's Be Friends

Choices for Rereading

Exploring Language Patterns

LAB, p. 107

To help children note the language pattern of the song, print the second verse on chart paper. Point out that the first and third lines are the same. Underline the words *three-wheel bikes,* and have children count how many times these words are repeated. (four) Then invite children to read the verse along with you as you point to the words.

You may want to reread all the verses, motioning for children to join you as you say the repeated words in each verse.

Have children complete *Literacy Activity Book* page 107.

Cooperative Reading

Provide partners with copies of the Little Big Book. Encourage children to read the story cooperatively, using the pictures as prompts. Suggest that children read alternate pages of text. Or, have one child read the beginning of the story, one read the middle, and the two of them choral read the ending.

Students Acquiring English Pair students acquiring English with more proficient English readers. Suggest that children acquiring English chime in on the repeated words and phrases.

Singing the Song

After teaching children the melody, invite them to sing the story with you, pointing to the words in the Big Book as you sing.

Acting Out the Song

To encourage creative expression, have children pantomime the activities as you read the verses. Or, invite children to sing the song with you as they pantomime the actions, using the pictures in the story as prompts.

Informal Assessment

Use Story Talk or the dramatization activity to assess children's general understanding of the story. Also, note children's ability to read cooperatively.

Responding

Responding to the Story

Story Talk

Place children in groups of two or three, and have them respond to one or more of the following:

- Does this story tell about real children or make-believe children? How do you know?

- Think about the story *Me Too!* How are the brother and sister in this story different from the brother and sister in *Me Too!*?

- Do you think a brother and sister can be friends? Why or why not?

Pantomime

Invite pairs of children to role play the brother and little sister in the story. Have them choose a picture card, name the activity, tell if it happened after breakfast or after lunch, and pantomime the scene. As the partners pantomime the scene, have children watching sing the verse that describes their actions.

Materials

- back packs
- picture cards to represent the activities in the story

Retelling *What Shall We Do When We All Go Out?*

Invite pairs of children to take turns retelling the story, using the retelling pieces and the prop board. Have a girl and a boy pretend they are the girl and the boy in the story. Ask them to place the pieces in the appropriate places on the board as they retell the story.

Materials

- Story Retelling Props pieces and prop board (See Teacher's Handbook, page H2.)

Home Connection

Invite children to draw their favorite scene from the story. Suggest that children take the pictures home and use them to retell, or sing, the story to their families. Suggest that children show their families how to change the verses to describe activities their family likes to do together.

Instruct *and* Integrate

Comprehension

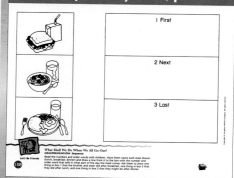

Practice Activities

Story Sequence

Extra Support Reread the story with children, having them raise their hands when they hear a word or group of words that tell *when* the brother and sister do something. Encourage children to tell how these words can help them figure out when things happen in a story. You might wish to help children retell the story by noting what the children do *after* breakfast and *after* lunch. Prompt children as needed by supplying the signal word and having children tell what happens:

> After Lunch
> First: The children feed the ducks.
> Next: They fly their kites.
> Then: They climb a tree.
> Last: They play hide-and-seek.

Using Words That Tell When

Ask children to talk about things they do in the morning, before having breakfast. Have them draw three pictures to show their ideas. Ask volunteers to display their drawings in the order in which the activities are done. Suggest that children use words such as *first*, *next*, *then*, and *last* or *before* and *after* to tell about their pictures. You may wish to display your own pictures and say, for example: The *first* thing I do *in the morning* is brush my teeth. *After* I brush my teeth, I get dressed. *Then* I make my bed.

Sequence Picture Puzzles

LAB, p. 108

Using simple line art, prepare a series of pictures that children can arrange in order to show what happens first, next, and last. For example:

- snowman base; base with head; finished snowman

After children have ordered the pictures, encourage them to use the pictures to tell a *first, next,* and *last* story. To provide more practice with sequence, have children complete *Literacy Activity Book* page 108.

Informal Assessment

As children complete the activities, note

- how well they are able to identify and use signal words and time markers to show sequence.
- their ability to identify words that begin with the sound for *f.*

Phonics/Decoding

Practice Activities

Literacy Activity Book, p. 109

Reading *f* Words

Extra Support Display Picture Cards *hook, fox,* and *feather*. Name the pictures with children. Explain that you are going to say a sentence and leave out a word. Children should supply the word by saying the picture name that makes sense and begins with the sound for *f*.

Read: *I have a ____ in my hat.*

Discuss why *feather* is the correct choice and why *fox* and *hook* are not. Then repeat the procedure with Picture Cards *four, five,* and *seven* and this sentence: *A hand has ____fingers.* (five)

Materials

- Picture Cards: *feather, four, fox, five, hook, seven*

My Big Dictionary

My Big Dictionary

Display page 15 of *My Big Dictionary*. Read the words *farmer, firefighter, fish,* and *football* aloud to children, pointing to the initial *f* and emphasizing the /f/ sound as you read. Invite partners to work together to draw three other things that begin with the sound for *f*. You may want to encourage children to use temporary spellings to label their drawings and make a list of their words for their Journals.

7

Hide-and-Seek *F*

LAB, p. 109

Have children complete *Literacy Activity Book* page 109 to practice identifying words that begin with the sound for *f*.

Extra Support After completing the page, invite children to work with partners to name and compare the hidden /f/ pictures they found.

Home Connection Invite children to bring *Literacy Activity Book* page 109 home to share with their families.

Portfolio Opportunity

- Save the *Literacy Activity Book* page to assess children's understanding of sequence.
- Save children's drawings of words beginning with *f* as a record of their ability to recognize words beginning with the sound for *f*.

3

Instruct
and
Integrate

Phonics/Decoding

Practice Activities

From Start to Finish

Invite small groups of children to play Friendship Fun, a beginning sound game.

- Name the pictures on the game board with children.

- Have children take turns spinning the spinner, naming the letter shown, and finding a picture on the board with a name that begins with the sound of the indicated letter.

- If a correct match is made, place a token over the picture.

- Play continues until all the pictures are covered. The player with the most tokens on the board wins.

Materials
- Game: Friendship Fun (See Teacher's Handbook, page H6.)

Feed the Ducks

 Extra Support Prepare a sock puppet to resemble a duck. Remind children that the brother and sister feed the ducks in the story. Tell children that they will now have a chance to feed a duck. Give the Picture Cards and sock puppet to a small group of children. Have children take turns trying to feed the duck. The child wearing the sock puppet should accept, or eat, only the Picture Cards whose names begin with the sound for *f*.

Materials
- Picture Cards: *fan, feather, feet, fence, fish, five, fork, four, fox,* along with several distracters
- duck sock puppet

Beginning Sound Riddles

 Challenge Provide small groups of children with Picture Cards that represent the beginning sounds they have learned so far. Have children take turns choosing a Picture Card, naming it silently to themselves, and providing clues for other group members to guess the name of the Picture Card. Children should begin with the clue that names the beginning sound, then keep providing more clues until the picture name is guessed. For example:

I begin with the sound for *f*.
I am an animal.
I live in the water. *(fish)*

Materials
- Picture Card

Informal Assessment

- As children complete the Phonics activities, note the ease with which they are able to recognize and identify /f/ words.

- As children listen and read the story, note their ability to read words from left to right.

Concepts About Print

Practice Activities

Reading Left to Right

Extra Support Remind children that the words on a page should be read in a certain order. Display the poster "With a Friend," and reread it with children. Call on a volunteer to point to the words in the first line, in order, as you read them aloud with children. Have another child repeat the procedure for the second line, another for the third, and so on, until the entire poem is read.

Recognizing Word Order in a Sentence

Have children work with partners to create sentences using the Word and Picture Cards. Observe children to see that they build their sentences, and read them, from left to right.

> **Materials**
> - Picture Cards
> - Word Cards

Listen and Read— Left to Right

Audio Tape for Let's Be Friends: *What Shall We Do When We All Go Out?*

Invite partners to listen to the tape as they follow the words in the Little Big Book. Suggest that children take turns running their fingers under the words as they read along to reinforce the left-to-right progression of the words.

3

THEME: LET'S BE FRIENDS

Instruct *and* Integrate

Vocabulary

Materials

- Picture Cards: *bathtub, bed, boat, car, desk, door, fork, garden, jeep, lamp, mirror, newspaper, piano, rug, sink, table, telephone, tent, van, wagon, window*

Informal Assessment

- As children complete the activities, note how easily they are able to recognize and read the high-frequency words.
- As children complete the Listening Activities, note their ability to listen and follow directions.

Practice Activities

Creating Sentences with *in*

LAB, p. 110

Extra Support Display the Picture Cards along the chalkboard ledge and have them named. Then display the following sentences in a pocket chart, allowing a space for a Picture Card as shown:

I go in a [_____].

I have a [_____] in my [house].

Have partners read the sentences and complete them by placing Picture Cards in the chart. Encourage children to try making new sentences by using different Picture Cards. Have children choose one of their sentences and draw a picture about it. Have children copy the sentence they illustrated below their pictures.

Have children complete *Literacy Activity Book* page 110.

What's in the Backpack?

Place the Word Cards children know in a child's empty backpack. Have children work with partners to draw a card from the backpack, read it, and use it in an oral sentence.

Challenge Suggest that children try to create oral sentences that tell about the story.

Word Memory

Invite partners to play Word Memory.

- Children mix up the Word Cards and place them face down on a desk or table top to form a 4 x 4 grid.

- Partners take turns turning over two cards, reading the words, and telling if the words are the same.

- If a child makes a match, the words are removed from play. If a match is not made, the cards are returned to the table top.

- Play continues until all the cards are matched.

Listening

Practice Activities

Finger Friends

Invite children to learn a finger rhyme. Repeat the following rhyme several times, until children are able to recite it on their own. Then teach children the actions that accompany the rhyme.

I have two friends
(hold up two fingers on left hand)

And they have me.
(hold up one finger on right hand)

Two friends and me,
(bend each from left to right)

That's 1, 2, 3.
(hold up fingers one at a time while saying 1, 2, 3)

Play "Simon Says"

Play Simon Says to practice words that tell *when* and promote careful listening. Explain that you will give a set of directions for children to follow. They are to only follow the directions Simon *says*: For example:

- Simon says, "Touch your toes *after* you touch your nose."

- Simon says, "*First* bark like a dog, then quack like a duck."

- "Hop on one foot, then the other."

- Simon says, "Put your hands in the air *before* you wave them."

- "Turn around in a circle three times, then sit down."

Listen and Read

 Audio Tape for Let's Be Friends: *What Shall We Do When We All Go Out?*

To promote careful listening and independent reading, invite children to listen to the tape as they follow the story in the Little Big Book.

Portfolio Opportunity

For a record of children's understanding of the high-frequency word *in*, save children's drawings of their sentences.

Instruct
and
Integrate

Oral Language

Choices for Oral Language

What a Day!

Challenge Recall with children that the brother and sister in the story "will think about tomorrow" as they eat their dinner. Mention to children that families do talk about what they will do tomorrow at dinner, but they also ask each other questions to find out what they did during the day.

Invite children to work in groups of three to four to role-play the brother and sister in the story and their parent(s). Encourage those playing the brother and sister to tell about the things they did. Suggest that those playing parents ask questions to learn more about the activities.

Things We Do in School

Reread the class story "What Shall We Do When We Go to School," page T37, with children. Using ideas from the story, help children begin a word web to tell when they do things throughout the day. Discuss the word web with children, asking which activities they enjoy most and why.

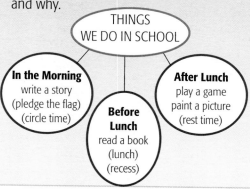

THINGS WE DO IN SCHOOL

In the Morning
write a story
(pledge the flag)
(circle time)

Before Lunch
read a book
(lunch)
(recess)

After Lunch
play a game
paint a picture
(rest time)

How Shall We Welcome a New Friend?

Discuss with children what they might do to welcome a new child into the class. Talk about how a new classmate might feel, eliciting thoughts such as *lonely* and *needing a friend*. Then have children brainstorm things they could do to welcome this child and make him or her know that they want to be friends.

Informal Assessment

- As children complete the Oral Language activities, note the ease with which they participate in group discussions.
- As children work on their writing assignments, note their use of correct directional patterns.

 # Writing

Choices for Writing

Autograph Book

Provide each child with several pieces of drawing paper. Show children how to fold the papers in half and staple them along the fold to create autograph books. Tell children to write their own names on the book cover. Then set aside some time each day for children to exchange and sign each other's books. Children may enjoy drawing small pictures by their names. You might model this by writing your own name and placing a heart or smiling face beside it.

My Friends at School

 Extra Support Help children create a bulletin board display entitled "My Friends at School." Using an instant camera, photograph each child. Attach the photographs to the bulletin board. Then provide children with index cards. Encourage children to write their full names on the index cards, providing assistance as needed. Have children post their names under the pictures.

Planning the Day

 Challenge Mention that many people make lists to plan their day. Encourage children to review the story to look for word and picture clues that tell what the brother and sister plan to do throughout the day.

Invite children to work with partners to list things they might do together. Have children choose a setting, such as a park, a school, or an arcade, and then plan their day.

Portfolio Opportunity

You might wish to save children's lists from Planning the Day for a writing sample.

3 Instruct *and* Integrate

Cross-Curricular Activities

Music/Movement

What Shall We Do When We Follow the Leader?

Tell children that *What Shall We Do When We All Go Out?* is a "Follow the Leader" game in which children sing the actions of the leader as they play. Teach children how to play, or have children tell how to play, Follow the Leader. Then invite children to use the language pattern from the story to sing about following the leader as they play.

What shall we do when we follow the leader,
follow the leader, follow the leader?
What shall we do when we follow the leader
When we all go out to play?
We will...

hip-hop on one foot	zig-zag all around
walk a straight line	clap our hands
walk like a duck	skip and jump

Art

Make a Collage

Revisit the story to talk about Shari Halpern's art. Explain that Ms. Halpern cuts out shapes from painted paper and photocopies of fabric and glues them onto paper to make her designs. Have children point out examples of painted paper and examples of fabric copies in the art.

Then invite children to create their own picture collages. Suggest that children work with simple shapes and designs. If children need help thinking of a subject, you might suggest the following: a boat, a house, a car, a bowl of fruit, a bird, a tree.

Materials
- construction paper
- bits of colored tissue paper, fabric, ribbons
- scissors
- glue

Social Studies

Taking Care of Our School

Remind children that after their picnic, the children in the story picked up their things and threw away their trash. Ask children to talk about the importance of keeping our play areas—parks, playgrounds, schoolyards, and so on—clean and safe so others can enjoy them.

Have children brainstorm in small groups to come up with ideas of how they might take care of these areas. Provide each group with materials to create posters that illustrate their ideas. You might arrange to display the posters in the school cafeteria or in other prominent spots around the school.

Science

Creating a Seesaw

Challenge Invite children to make tiny seesaws by taping a pencil to a table top and balancing a ruler across the pencil. Encourage children to experiment with the seesaw to draw their own conclusions about how one works. Suggest that children:

1 Place two or three coins on one end of the ruler to see what happens.

2 Add coins to the other end to see if they can balance it again.

3 Move one stack of coins toward the center of the ruler to see what happens.

Talk about children's findings. Help them draw conclusions about riding on a seesaw with a parent or with someone their own size.

Materials
- a pencil with flat surfaces (a ruler will slide off a round pencil)
- a stiff wooden ruler
- masking tape
- coins or tokens

BIG BOOK

SELECTION:
Together

Big Book

Little Big Book

by George Ella Lyon
illustrated by Vera Rosenberry

Other Books
by George Ella Lyon

A B Cedar: An Alphabet of Trees
Come a Tide
Dreamplace

Selection Summary

In this rhyming story, two friends can do almost anything—build a house, make ice cream, fight a fire, especially if they do it together.

Lesson Planning Guide

	Skill/Strategy Instruction	Meeting Individual Needs	Lesson Resources
1 Introduce *the* Literature *Pacing: 1 day*	**Shared Reading and Writing** Warm-up/Build Background, T68 Shared Reading, T68 Shared Writing, T69	Choices for Rereading, T69	**Poster** The More We Get Together, T68 *Literacy Activity Book* Personal Response, p. 111
2 Interact *with* Literature *Pacing: 1-2 days*	**Reading Strategies** Self-Question, T70 Monitor, T70 Evaluate, T72, T76, T82 Summarize, T76, T82 Think About Words, T78 **Minilessons** ✔ Initial *p*, T73 ✔ Noting Details, T75 ✔ High-Frequency Words: *put*, T77 ✔ Phonogram *-ig*, T79 ✔ Beginning of a Sentence, T81	**Students Acquiring English**, T70, T74, T84 **Extra Support**, T73 **Challenge**, T80 **Rereading and Responding**, T84–T85	**Letter, Word, and Picture Cards**, T73, T77, T79 *Literacy Activity Book* Language Patterns, p. 112 See the Houghton Mifflin **Internet** resources for additional activities.
3 Instruct *and* Integrate *Pacing: 1-2 days*	**Reading/Listening Center**, Comprehension, T86 Phonics/Decoding, T87–T88 Concepts About Print, T89 Vocabulary, T90 Listening, T91 **Independent Reading & Writing**, T92–T93 **Language/Writing Center**, Oral Language, T94 Writing, T95 **Cross-Curricular Center**, Cross-Curricular Activities, T96–T97	**Challenge**, T88, T91, T95, T96 **Extra Support**, T86, T87, T88, T89, T90, T94 **Students Acquiring English**, T94	**Poster** Friendly Puppets, T89 With a Friend, T89 **Letter, Word, and Picture Cards**, T87, T88 **My Big Dictionary**, T87 *Literacy Activity Book* Comprehension, p. 113 Phonics/Decoding, pp. 114, 115 Vocabulary, p. 116 Tear-and-Take, pp. 117-118 **Audio Tape** for Let's Be Friends: *Together* See the Houghton Mifflin **Internet** resources for additional activities.

✔ *Indicates Tested Skills. See page T11 for assessment options.*

Introduce *the* Literature

Shared Reading and Writing

Poster

THE MORE WE GET TOGETHER

The more we get together, together, together.
The more we get together, the happier we'll be.
'Cause your friends are my friends,
And my friends are your friends,
The more we get together, the happier we'll be.

Song Tape for Let's Be Friends:
"The More We Get Together"

Literacy Activity Book, p. 111

INTERACTIVE LEARNING

Warm-up/Build Background

Sharing a Song
- Display the poster "The More We Get Together."
- Invite children to listen and follow along as you play the tape for *"The More We Get Together."* (For lyrics and music see Teacher's Handbook, page H12.)
- Point to and read the last line on the poster. Invite children to talk about how happy being together with their friends makes them feel.
- Then play the song again, inviting children to sing along.

Shared Reading
LAB, p. 111

Preview and Predict
- Display *Together* and read the title. Point to the names of the author and illustrator and read them for children.
- Briefly discuss the cover illustration. Note that the two friends seem to have jumped up from the water and are hanging from the letters in the title. Ask if this could really happen or if it is make believe.
- Display and read aloud pages 6-13 and ask children what they think the story will be about. You might model with a Think Aloud.

Think Aloud
The title and the other pictures in the story tell me that it will be about two friends who like to play and make believe together. I wonder what other things they will do?

- Encourage children to predict what other things the two friends might do together.

Read Together
- Invite children to read the story with you, joining in on the rhyming words and any other words they know.
- Pause for children to comment on the illustrations and to match their predictions to what happens in the story.

Personal Response
Invite children to share some of the make-believe games they like to play with friends. Then have children complete *Literacy Activity Book* page 111 to draw and write about a make-believe thing they'd like to do with a friend.

Shared Writing: *A Class Story*

Brainstorming   Note that while the two friends do many make-believe things together, children do many real things together in class each day. Brainstorm with them a list of real things they do with their classmates.

read a book
paint a picture
build with blocks

Drafting   Read through the list with children. Invite them to contribute sentences to the class story. As you write the sentences on chart paper, encourage children to supply the initial consonant of words whose beginning sounds they have learned. Also, point out the use of a capital letter to begin the first word of each sentence.

Publishing   Write each line on separate sheets of drawing paper. Have volunteers illustrate the scenes. Then bind the pages together to make a book entitled *Things We Do Together* for the Reading/Listening Center.

Choices for Rereading

Rereadings provide varied experiences with the literature, enabling children to make its language and content their own. The following rereading choices appear on page T84.

- Vocabulary Development
- Exploring Language Patterns
- Partner Reading
- Echo Reading

Interact
with
Literature

You cut the timber
and I'll build the house.

6

You bring the cheese
and I'll fetch the mouse.

8

Visual Literacy

Direct attention to the storefronts. Note the word written on one shop and the symbol hanging above it. Help children identify the symbol and then call on a volunteer to read the word. *(cheese)*

Vocabulary

Word Meaning If necessary, tell children what *fetch* means. (to go get) They may know the word in the context of a dog fetching a ball. Encourage them to show how the friend fetches the mouse.

Background: FYI

This "Pied Piper" seems to be leading the mice into town. Some children may know of the original Pied Piper who lured the rats of Hamelin out of town.

Interact *with* Literature

Reading Strategies

 Evaluate

Student Application Invite children to describe the picture on page 11. Encourage them to tell whether or not this picture makes sense and why. Ask how knowing that the girls are using their imaginations as they work and play makes it easier to understand the page.

Encourage their reactions to the picture on pages 12 and 13. Ask children if they think it would be more fun to imagine eating a huge banana split like this than eating a small one.

You salt the ice
and I'll crank the cream.

10

Let's put our heads together

12

QuickREFERENCE

Science Link

Note that a real ice-cream maker is much smaller than the one in the picture. Then tell children how ice cream is made: cream and other ingredients are placed in the machine and surrounded with ice and salt. The cream is mixed until it freezes.

Visual Literacy

Have children name other things the girls used to make ice cream. Read the words *vanilla* and *sugar*. Note the berries and ask what kind of ice cream the girls might be making. (strawberry)

Vocabulary

Word Meaning Tell children that *crank* is both a doing and a naming word. The handle on the ice-cream machine is called a *crank*; the word we use to tell what someone does when they turn the handle is also *crank*.

and dream the same dream.

Big Book pp. 11, 13

MINILESSON

Phonics/Decoding

Initial *p*

Teach/Model

Display Magic Picture *pig*.

Have children name the picture, listening for the beginning sound. Note that Magic Picture *pig* helps them remember the sound for *p*.

Display pages 12-13 of the story. Ask children to listen as you read aloud the sentence. Have them listen for a word that begins with the sound for *p*. *(put)*

Practice/Apply

Repeat the procedure with the sentences on page 22 and 24. Call on volunteers to frame the words *pail* and *paint* respectively. Have the initial consonant *p* named in each word.

SKILL FINDER Reading *p* Words, page T87

MEETING INDIVIDUAL NEEDS Extra Support

Contractions The contraction *Let's* is a shorter way of saying *Let us*. Note that the word *Let's* also appears in the theme title.

Vocabulary

Idioms Tell children that the phrase *put our heads together* means to plan or talk about things together. Have partners pantomime putting their heads together to discuss a plan.

Journal

As children read, have them write or draw to make a list of each thing the girls do together. Children can use the lists to summarize the story.

Interact *with* Literature

BIG BOOK

I'll drive the truck
if you'll fight the fire.

14

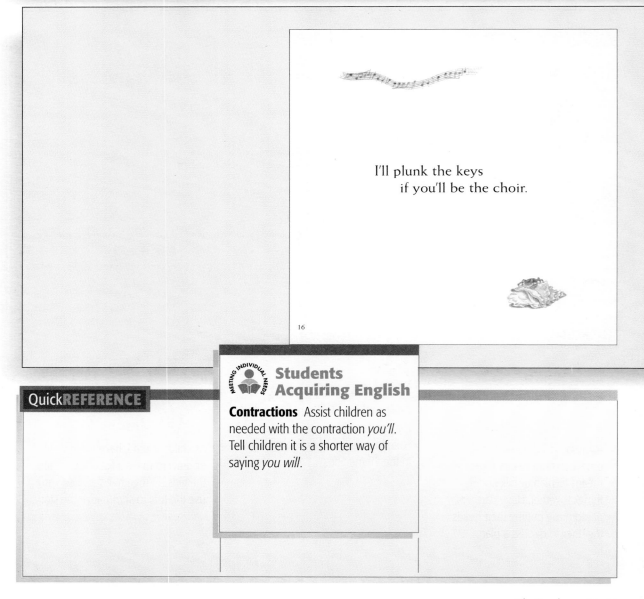

I'll plunk the keys
if you'll be the choir.

16

QuickREFERENCE

Students Acquiring English

Contractions Assist children as needed with the contraction *you'll*. Tell children it is a shorter way of saying *you will*.

MINILESSON

Comprehension

Noting Details

TESTED SKILL

Teach/Model

Ask children what they notice about each page of the story. (Each page tells a different way the girls work and play together.) Mention to children that they can use clues in the words and the pictures to learn more about the ways the girls share their work and play.

Think Aloud

When I read, I look for clues in the words and pictures to help me understand what I am reading. The picture on page 15 shows how the girls play at putting out the fire. The words tell me that one girl will drive the truck and that the other will fight the fire.

Ask children to use word and picture clues to tell who the *I* is on this page. (the girl driving the truck) Ask who the *you* is. (the girl fighting the fire)

Practice/Apply

Invite children to use picture clues to tell what is happening on pages 16-17.

SKILL FINDER

Noting Details About Character's Actions, page T86

Minilessons, Themes 1, 3, and 6

Visual Literacy

Point out the musical notes at the top of page 16. Ask if children have seen anything like this before. Explain that the circles and lines are called *notes* and that people read the notes to help them play musical instruments.

Vocabulary

Word Meaning Ask children what the girl plunks in the picture on page 17. (different things she's found on the beach) Mention that a *choir* is a group of singers.

Science Link

Encourage children to tell what they know about beaches. To prompt discussion, have them identify items in the picture they might see at a beach. (waves, shells, driftwood, and crabs)

Interact
with
Literature

Reading Strategies

▶ **Summarize**
Evaluate

Student Application Ask children to tell what this story is about. (two girls who use their imaginations when they work and play together) Have children name some of the things the girls do together. If children have been recording these activities in their journals, encourage them to use their lists to summarize the story through page 21.

Ask if children would like to be friends with these girls. Encourage them to tell why or why not.

BIG BOOK

I'll find the ball
if you'll call the team.

18

Let's put our heads together

20

QuickREFERENCE

Vocabulary

Word Meaning Children may know the word *team* in the context of a group of players. But if they look at the picture, they'll see the girl is referring to a team of horses.

★☆★ Multicultural Link

Explain that two-wheeled chariots like the one on page 20 were often used for racing. Chariot racing was a popular sport in ancient Rome.

and dream the same dream.

21

Big Book pp. 19, 21

MINILESSON

High-Frequency Words: *put*

TESTED SKILL

Teach/Model

Display Word Card *put* and read the word aloud. Ask what sound children hear at the beginning of the word. (/p/) Ask what letter stands for this sound. *(p)*

Reread the sentence on pages 20-21, saying "blank" for the word *put*. Ask children to read the word. Invite children to compare the Word Card *put* to the word *put* on page 20 letter for letter.

Practice/Apply

Use Word and Picture Cards to construct this sentence:

I put the [ball] in the [garden].

Read the sentence with children, asking a volunteer to frame the word *put*. Invite children to find the ball in the garden on page 19.

SKILL FINDER — Play the Hokey Pokey, page T90

Visual Literacy

Challenge children to find the ball and team on pages 20-21. (the sun and the horses pulling the chariot) Help them make the connection between this spread and pages 18-19.

Interact with Literature

BIG BOOK

You dig for water
and I'll make a pail.

22

Reading Strategies

▶ **Think About Words**

Discuss how children could figure out the word *boat* on page 24.

The story says: *I'll paint the ___ if you'll set the sail.*

- **What makes sense** This word names something that can be painted.

- **Sounds for letters** The word begins with the letter *b*.

- **Picture clues** I see one of the girls setting the sail and the other girl painting a boat in the picture. When I say the word *boat,* I hear the sound for *b* at the beginning. The word must be *boat*.

Have children reread the sentence on page 24 with you. Ask if the word *boat* makes sense.

I'll paint the boat
if you'll set the sail.

24

QuickREFERENCE

Science Link

Tell children that people do indeed dig for water. Ask if children have ever seen a well or read about one. Tell children that to get water from a well, people lower a pail or bucket into the water in the well and then pull the pail full of water back up.

Phonics/Decoding Review

As you reread page 22, ask children to listen for a word that begins with the sound for *p. (pail)* Repeat the procedure for the word *paint* on page 24.

Phonics/Decoding

Phonogram -ig

TESTED SKILL

Teach/Model

Display Magic Picture *pig*, reviewing that it helps children remember the sound for *p*.

Then read aloud page 22, asking children to listen for a word that rhymes with *pig*. *(dig)* Write *pig* and *dig* on the chalkboard, one beneath the other.

Think Aloud

When I look at the words *pig* and *dig*, the first thing I notice is that they begin with different letters. I also notice that they have two letters that are the same, the letters *ig*.

Explain that children can use what they know about the beginning sounds to read new words that end with *ig*. Add *big* to the list of words on the chalkboard. Call on a volunteer to read the word aloud.

Practice/Apply

Display these sentences.

I dig.
I have a big pig.

Ask children to use what they know about the sounds for *b*, *d*, and *p* to read the sentences.

SKILL FINDER

Spelling Words with *-ig*, page T88

Vocabulary

Word Meaning Children may know the word *set* in the context of setting a table or in naming a group of things. Tell children that here the word *set* means "to put up" the sail of the boat.

BIG BOOK

You catch the fish
and I'll catch the stream!

26

Let's put our heads together

28

QuickREFERENCE

Social Studies Link

Note how the girl "catches" the stream on page 27. Explain that people do block rivers or streams to collect water. Ask children what would happen if a river were dammed, or blocked up. (The water would have no place to go; it would collect to form a lake.)

 Challenge

Point out that the fish on page 26 are found in a stream. Ask children what other places fish are found. (river, ocean, pond)

and dream the same dream.

29

Concepts About Print:

Beginning of a Sentence

TESTED SKILL

Teach/Model

Read aloud pages 28-29, pointing to each word. Remind children that a word is a group of letters with a little extra space on either side. Ask children to help you count the words on the spread. (ten) Then use a Think Aloud to help children find the beginning of the sentence.

Think Aloud

A sentence is a group of *words* that tells about someone or something. A sentence has clues that tell me where it begins. The first word in a sentence always begins with a capital letter. (point to *Let's*) This word begins with a capital letter, a capital *L*, so it must be the first word in the sentence.

Read the sentence with children.

Practice/Apply

Display pages 28 and 29 and read them with children. Ask children to find and frame the first word in the sentence. Verify with children that the word begins with a capital letter.

SKILL FINDER

Recognizing Sentence Beginnings, page T89

Visual Literacy

Help children make the connection between pages 26-27 and pages 28-29 by asking them what became of the fish and the stream. (The girls are riding the fish; the stream has become an ocean.)

Big Book pp. 27, 29

Interact
with
Literature

Reading Strategies

▶ **Summarize**
Evaluate

Student Application Tell children that good readers think about the most important parts of a story to help them remember it. They also tell whether or not they liked a story. Encourage children to take turns retelling the story and telling how they feel about it.

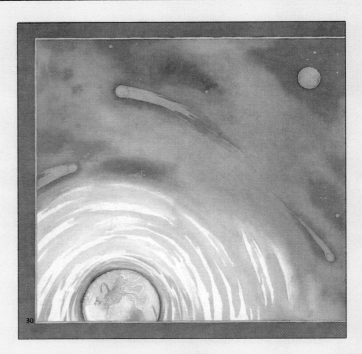

BIG BOOK

30

Self-Assessment

Have children ask themselves:

● Can I retell this story to a friend?
● Can I tell someone how I feel about this story?

 **Journal**

Invite children to draw their favorite scene from the story. Have them talk about why it was their favorite scene.

Interact with Literature

Rereading

Literacy Activity Book, p. 112

You _____
and I'll _____

Informal Assessment

- Use Story Talk or the retelling activity to assess children's general understanding of *Together*.
- As children read on their own, note their ability to move from the front to the back of the book.

Choices for Rereading

Vocabulary Development

As you reread the story with children, pause now and then to help them focus attention on selection vocabulary. Ask children to listen for a word that:

- page 6: names wood for a house (timber)

- page 8: means "to get" (fetch)

- page 10: means "to turn" (crank)

- page 16: means "to tap, hit" (plunk)

- page 18: names a group of players (team)

- page 22: means the same as bucket (pail)

Exploring Language Patterns

LAB, p. 112

Read the story, focusing attention on the language pattern used to describe how the two friends share their work and play. Note with children that these pages follow one of two patterns:

I'll ____ if you'll ____.
You ____ and I'll ____.

Have children complete *Literacy Activity Book* page 112.

Echo Reading

Students Acquiring English
To promote fluency, read aloud each spread of the story, and then have children read the spread aloud. Emphasize the rhythm and rhyme, encouraging children to follow your example.

Partner Reading

Provide partners with a copy of the Little Big Book. Encourage them to read the story cooperatively, using the pictures as prompts. Partners might take turns reading alternate pages of text. Or, one child might read the main text with the second reading the lines that repeat.

Responding

Choices for Responding

Story Talk

Place children in groups of two or three, and have them respond to the following:

- Which make-believe activity do the two friends do that you would also like to do?

- Do you think these friends also enjoy doing real things together?

- How is this story like *What Shall We Do When We All Go Out?* How is it different?

Retelling *Together*

Invite children to use stanza boards to retell *Together*. Encourage them to tell how the two friends share their work and play.

Materials
- oak tag
- crayons or markers
- scissors
- glue

(See Teacher's Handbook, page H3.)

Add New Scenes

Invite children to think of other make-believe things the two friends might do together. List their suggestions on the chalkboard. Then invite children to draw and write about their ideas.

Home Connection

Encourage children to draw their favorite scene from the story, copying the line of text beneath their pictures. Suggest that they share their drawings with their families to retell the story. Children might also discuss with family members things they like to do together.

Portfolio Opportunity

- Save *Literacy Activity Book* page 112 as a record of children's understanding of language pattern in the story.

- Save children's drawings of new scenes as a record of children's response to the story.

Instruct *and* **Integrate**

Comprehension

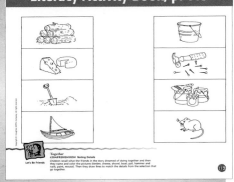

Literacy Activity Book, p. 113

Practice Activities

Noting Details About Characters' Actions

LAB, p. 113

Extra Support Invite children to reread the story with you. Ask them to use word and picture clues to tell more about each thing the girls do and how they share their work and play. Note that on many pages, the roles of *you* and *I* are reversed, as the girls also take turns "speaking." Encourage children to use picture details to identify the "I" and "you" on each page.

Have children complete *Literacy Activity Book* page 113.

Identifying Characters' Feelings

Note with children that the words in the story don't say how the girls feel about what they are doing. Invite children to look at the pictures for clues that tell how the girls feel when they are together. Suggest that children draw pictures to show how they feel when they work and play with their friends. Encourage them to share their drawings with the class and tell something about them.

What Would You Do?

Ask children to think about their favorite part of the story. Which activity would they most enjoy doing? Have children draw and write about their choice. Suggest that they include picture details to show how they would share the work with a friend. Encourage children to share their ideas with the class.

Noting Details About Setting

Ask children to think about the story *Where Does the Brown Bear Go?* Recall that this story has many different places where the characters go, just as *Together* does. Reread *Where Does the Brown Bear Go?* to review these places with children. Then have them work in small groups to name the places shown in *Together*.

Informal Assessment

As children complete the activities on these pages, note their ability to identify details in the words and pictures and to read words beginning with *p*.

Phonics/Decoding

Practice Activities

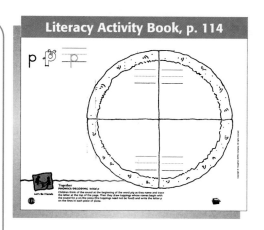

Reading *P* Words

LAB, p. 114

Extra Support Display Picture Cards *waffle, pancakes,* and *pizza.* Name the pictures with children. Explain that you are going to say a sentence that tells something the two girls might do together and leave out a word. Children should supply the word by saying the picture name that makes sense and begins with the sound for p. Read: I'll get the syrup and you'll get the ____.

Discuss why *pancakes* is the right choice and *waffle* and *pizza* are not. Then repeat the procedure with Picture Cards *guitar, piano,* and *paints: I'll sing the song and you'll play the ____.* (piano)

Have children complete *Literacy Activity Book* page 114

Materials
- Picture Cards: *guitar, paints, pancakes, piano, pizza, waffle*

My Big Dictionary

Display pages 26-27 of *My Big Dictionary*. Read the words aloud to children, pointing to the initial *p* and emphasizing the /p/ sound as you read. Invite partners to work together to find five things on page 27 that begin with the sound for *p*. You may want to encourage children to use temporary spellings and make a list of their words for their Journals.

You'll Cut and I'll Paste

Have children work with partners to make a collage of *p* words. Children should share the task, taking turns cutting /p/ pictures from magazines and pasting them onto paper. Encourage children to label the pictures they find.

My Big Dictionary

Portfolio Opportunity

Save *Literacy Activity Book* page 114 or children's writings from the other phonics activities as a record of their work.

Instruct *and* Integrate

Phonics/Decoding

Literacy Activity Book, p. 115

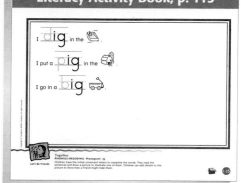

Practice Activities

Spelling Words with *-ig*

Extra Support Display Picture Card *pig*, and have it named. Show children how to use the Phonogram Card *-ig* and Letter Card *p* to make the word *pig*. Read the word with children.

Display Letter Cards *b* and *d* and Phonogram Card *-ig* along the chalkboard ledge. Then read aloud the following words and sentences. Have children construct and then write each word:

- *big:* I have a big boat.
- *dig:* I can dig a hole.
- *pig:* I can feed the pig.

Materials
- Picture Card: *pig*
- Letter Cards for *b, d,* and *p*
- Phonogram Card: *-ig*

Reading *-ig* Words

Provide partners with Letter Cards for *b, d,* and *p* and an index card that reads *ig*. Then invite children to work together to make three words that end with *ig*. Encourage children to list each word they make, then use it in an oral sentence.

Practice with *-ig*

LAB, p. 115

To provide practice with the phonogram *-ig*, have children complete *Literacy Activity Book* page 115.

Challenge Children may wish to work with partners to illustrate the sentences.

Informal Assessment

As children complete the activities,
- note their ability to identify the first word in a sentence.
- assess their ability to spell and read words with the phonogram *-ig*.

Concepts About Print

Practice Activities

Recognizing Sentence Beginnings

MEETING INDIVIDUAL NEEDS

Extra Support Display the poster "With a Friend," and invite children to reread it with you. Then point to the first verse with children. Ask how many lines they see in the first verse. (four) Then ask how many sentences they see. (one) As needed, remind children that they can tell the beginning of a sentence because it begins with a capital letter.

Repeat the procedure for each verse in the poem. Make sure children realize that the last verse has two sentences.

Poster

Friendly Puppets
Make a puppet of your friend.

1. Get ready.
2. Cut out and glue shapes.
3. Color the puppet.
4. Glue on a stick.

How Many Sentences?

Ask children to work with partners to find out how many sentences are in the story. As partners identify each sentence, have them make a tally mark on a piece of paper. Encourage partners to share their findings with the class. If partners fail to come up with the same number of sentences as other groups, repeat the activity with the whole group.

Reading Directions

Display the poster "Friendly Puppets." Invite children to read the directions for making the friendly puppets with you. Call on volunteers to point to the first word in each sentence as you read.

Then invite children to make their own friendly puppets. You will need the following to complete the activity: colored paper, crayons, pipe cleaners, scissors, tape, and glue.

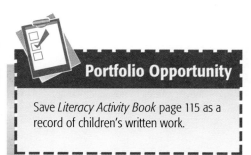

Portfolio Opportunity

Save *Literacy Activity Book* page 115 as a record of children's written work.

Instruct and Integrate

Vocabulary

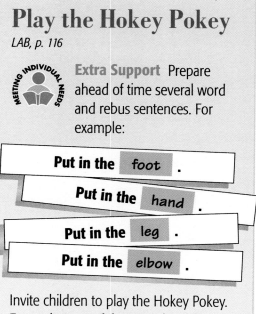
Practice Activities

Play the Hokey Pokey

LAB, p. 116

Extra Support Prepare ahead of time several word and rebus sentences. For example:

> Put in the foot .
> Put in the hand .
> Put in the leg .
> Put in the elbow .

Invite children to play the Hokey Pokey. For each verse of the song, have them take turns choosing and reading to find out what verse they will sing next.

Have children complete *Literacy Activity Book* page 116.

Put It All Away

Invite children to work together to clean the classroom at the end of the day. Prepare rebus sentence strips with tasks children should complete. Each child chooses a sentence, reads it, and completes that task. Discuss how quickly the classroom is cleaned up when everyone works together.

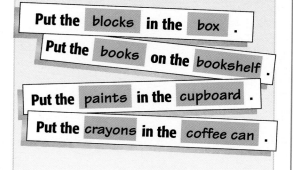

> Put the blocks in the box .
> Put the books on the bookshelf .
> Put the paints in the cupboard .
> Put the crayons in the coffee can .

You Read the Word and I'll Say a Sentence

Place high-frequency words children know in a small pail. Have children work together to read the words and use them in oral sentences. Suggest that children take turns choosing and reading a word for their partners to use in oral sentences.

Tear-and-Take Story

LAB, pp. 117-118

Have children remove the *Literacy Activity Book* page, fold it to make a book, and read the story.

Home Connection Then suggest that they take their books home and read them to family members.

The Fig Tree

Informal Assessment

- As children read the Tear-and-Take story and complete other activities, note how readily they are able to identify the high-frequency words.

- Observe children's listening skills as they "put their heads together" to brainstorm things they might do together.

Listening

Practice Activities

Let's Put Our Heads Together

- Partners put their heads together to brainstorm a list of real and imaginary tasks they might complete.

- They choose one task that they might complete together and talk about ways they could share the task.

- They draw about their ideas.

1. follow a rainbow
2. fly a kite
3. dig for treasure
4. wash a pet

Listen and Read!

 Audio Tape for Let's Be Friends: *Together*

Place copies of the Little Big Book along with the tape in the Reading/Listening Center. Have children follow along, listening for rhyming words and joining in on the lines and words that are the same.

Listening for Rhyming Words

Ask children to listen for rhyming words as you reread the story. As each set of rhyming words is identified, have children say the words after you, listening for the ending sounds.

Challenge Invite children to suggest additional rhyming words for each pair of story words.

Portfolio Opportunity

As children complete the Vocabulary activities, write down some observations about each child's ability to identify and understand *put*. Place these observations in their portfolios.

Instruct and Integrate

Independent Reading & Writing

Pig Pals

WATCH **ME** READ

Pig Pals
by Jeffrey Williams

This story provides practice and application for the following skills:

■ **High-Frequency Words:** *in, put*

■ **Phonics/Decoding Skills:** Initial *f* and *p*; phonogram *-ig*

■ **Cumulative Review:** Previously taught decoding skills and High-Frequency Words

INTERACTIVE LEARNING

Independent Reading
Watch Me Read

Preview and Predict
- Display *Pig Pals*. Read aloud the title and the names of the author and illustrator.
- Briefly discuss the cover, having children tell where the story takes place.
- Preview pages 1-7 and name each story character—Julio, Kim, Tom, Jessica—with children. Help them conclude from the pictures that it is Show-and-Tell time. Ask what all the children are showing. (pigs)
- Invite children to predict what Jessica's pig will be like.

Read the Story
- Ask children to read the story independently to find out if their predictions about Jessica's pig match the story.
- After reading ask:
  What kind of pig does Jessica have?
  How does Jessica's pig differ from the other pigs?

Rereading
- Have children work in groups of four to reread characters' lines. Suggest that children use picture clues to describe at least one more thing about the pig their character is showing.
- As children reread the story, have them note details in the words and pictures that help tell how the pigs are alike and different. Encourage children to talk about these similarities and differences in small groups.

Responding
- Invite children to draw and write about their favorite pigs from the story.
- Ask children to draw another pig pal for Pig Day. Suggest they use the story pattern to write about their pigs: *(Child's name) said, "I have a pig."*

Informal Assessment

- As children read aloud *Pig Pals* and complete other activities, note whether they begin to recognize the High-Frequency Words at sight.
- As children reread the story with partners, note whether they move from the front to the back of the book.
- As children complete the writing activities, assess their ability to draw to convey meaning.

Student Selected Reading

Book Buddies

If children hesitate in selecting and reading a book on their own, try this.

- Each week, designate two to three children to be "Book Buddies."

- Give these children special name tags and suggest titles they might help a friend read.

- At the start of a reading period, Book Buddies can be paired up with a class-mate who is having trouble finding and/or reading a book.

Let's Read It Together

Place the Big Books children have read so far in the Reading and Listening Center. Invite children to reread the books—together with a friend. Encourage children to think of different ways to share the reading of the stories:

- alternating pages of text

- choral reading

- echo reading

- a combination of the above

Student Selected Writing

Let's-Be-Friends Paper Dolls

Cut out a simple doll pattern so that when the paper is open, you have two paper dolls holding hands. Prepare a set of paper dolls for each child. Then have children

- write something they like to do with a friend on one doll,

- add features and clothes to the other to resemble themselves,

- display the dolls on the *A Friend Is…* bulletin board.

Word Banks

If children do not have their own word banks, encourage them to begin one at this time. Suggest that children bring in from home shoeboxes they can decorate to hold their words. As children come across a word they would like to add to their banks, help them spell the word on an index card. Invite children to illustrate the word or decorate the card any way they wish.

Books for Independent Reading

Pig Pals
by Jeffrey Williams

Children may also enjoy rereading the WATCH ME READ titles from earlier themes.

What Shall We Do When We All Go Out?
illustrated by Shari Halpern

Together
by George Ella Lyon
illustrated by Vera Rosenberry

Have children read these books independently or with a partner. Children may also enjoy rereading the Little Big Book titles from earlier themes.

See the Bibliography on pages T6–T7 for more theme-related books for independent reading.

Ideas for Independent Writing

- a **list** of things to do with a friend

- a **message** to a friend

- a **note** from one story character to another

Portfolio Opportunity

Save examples of the writing children do independently on self-selected topics.

Oral Language

Choices for Oral Language

What Goes Together?

Students Acquiring English Engage children in a conversation about things that go together. Then:

- Choose a topic, such as food, and have children brainstorm a list of food go-togethers.

- Have children work in mixed pairs to role play the go-togethers, for example, peanut butter and jelly, and to tell why they think they go so well together.

- Encourage classmates to ask the go-together pair questions about their relationship.

Food Go-Togethers	Clothes Go-Togethers
peanut butter and jelly	socks and shoes
cheese and crackers	hat and a scarf
bread and butter	raincoat and umbrella

How to Be a Good Friend

Have children think about the things that make a good friend. Then invite children to help you make a list of rules they can follow to be good friends. Record children's ideas on chart paper.

Have children illustrate the chart with examples, and display it in the classroom.

A Good Friend...
Listens to you
Shares
Makes you feel happy
Helps you

Playing Together

Extra Support Display pages 18-19 of the story and reread them with children. Ask children if they can name team games. Record their suggestions on the chalkboard.

Read through the list with children. Then invite them to tell what they know about each game on the list.

Team Games

baseball	basketball
soccer	kickball
football	hide-and-seek
relay	dodge ball

Informal Assessment

- As children complete the brainstorming activities on this page, note their level of oral participation.

- As children work on their friendship cards, note how well they write their own messages.

 # Writing

Choices for Writing

A Friendship Card

Provide children with construction paper, crayons, markers, ribbon, glitter, or other materials to make friendship cards for a special friend. Have children:

- decorate their cards any way they wish,

- write, or dictate, a message to their friend,

- share their cards with the class,

- give their cards to a classmate or a neighborhood friend.

Home Connection If children wish to make friendship cards for family members, permit them to do so.

Let's Put Our Heads Together

Challenge Remind children that when the two friends in the story put their heads together, they could dream the same dream. Invite children to work with partners to "dream the same dream." Have them work cooperatively to draw a picture of something they would like to do together. Encourage children to write a sentence to tell about their pictures.

Safety Posters

Recall that the two friends work together to put out a make-believe dragon's fire. Ask if children know how real fires happen. Encourage them to talk about things they can do to keep fires from starting and what they should do if they see a fire.

Invite children to take what they learned from the discussion and make fire safety posters. Children should draw and write about one thing children can do to help keep a fire from happening.

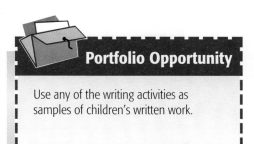

Portfolio Opportunity

Use any of the writing activities as samples of children's written work.

Instruct and Integrate

Cross-Curricular Activities

Music

Making Music

Ask children how the two friends made music on page 23. Ask if they have ever tried to make music by hitting different objects, such as pots and pans. Then invite children to make music in the classroom:

- Fill several drinking glasses with different levels of water.
- Line up the glasses so that each has just a little more water in it than the one next to it.
- Have children tap the glasses gently with a spoon.
- Talk about the different sounds they hear. Which glass of water makes the highest sound? Which makes the lowest?

Challenge Invite children to try tapping simple tunes on the water glasses such as the Theme Song "Make New Friends."

Materials
- several glasses
- water
- a spoon

Math

Our Favorite Ice Cream Flavors

Recall that the girls in the story made their own ice cream. Invite children to share their favorite ice-cream flavors with the class. Then help children record their selections on a graph. Your graph might resemble the following:

	1	2	3	4	5
Chocolate					
Vanilla					
Strawberry					
Chocolate Chip					

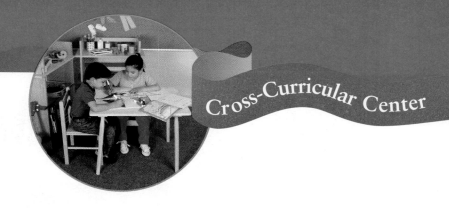

Art

Build a House

Provide partners with a handful of craft sticks and some glue to build their own houses. Before children begin, have them brainstorm ideas for how they will go about building their houses. You might suggest that children look at page 3 of the story for ideas.

Materials
- craft sticks
- glue or paste

Science

What Floats

Remind children that the two friends in a story sail a boat together. Tell children that a boat can go on the water because it floats. Then invite children to find things that float in the classroom.

1 Have children name each item and examine it.

2 Ask children to predict whether or not an item will float.

3 Place the item on the water, and have children observe what happens.

4 Help children draw conclusions about what they see.

5 Experiment placing the items into the water in different ways. For example, will a pencil float if it is placed lengthwise on the surface of the water? Will it float if it is placed into the water end first?

Materials
- a variety of floating and non-floating items
- a plastic tub of water or a water table

Theme Assessment Wrap-Up

ASSESSMENT

Reflecting/Self-Assessment

Copy the chart below to distribute to children. Ask them which stories in the theme they liked best. Then discuss what was easy for them and what was more difficult as they read the selections and completed the activities. Have children put a check mark under either *Easy* or *Hard*.

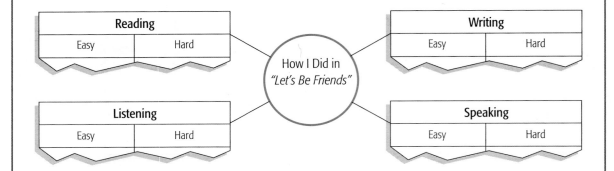

Reading	
Easy	Hard

Writing	
Easy	Hard

How I Did in
"Let's Be Friends"

Listening	
Easy	Hard

Speaking	
Easy	Hard

Monitoring Literacy Development

There will be many opportunities to observe and evaluate children's literacy development. As children participate in literacy activities, note whether each child has a beginning, a developing, or a proficient understanding of reading, writing, and language concepts. The Observation Checklists, which can be used for recording and evaluating this information, appear in the *Teacher's Assessment Handbook*. They are comprised of the following:

Concepts About Print and Book Handling Behaviors
- Concepts about print
- Book handling

Emergent Reading Behaviors
- Responding to literature
- Storybook rereading
- Decoding strategies

Emergent Writing Behaviors
- Writing
- Stages of Temporary Spelling

Oral Language Behaviors
- Listening attentively
- Listening for information
- Listening to directions
- Listening to books
- Speaking/language development
- Participating in conversations and discussions

Retelling Behaviors
- Retelling a story
- Retelling informational text

Portfolio Opportunity

Invite children to save one piece of work that they did during "Let's Be Friends."

Choices for Assessment

Informal Assessment

Review the Observation Checklists and observation notes to determine:

- Did children's responses during and after reading indicate comprehension of the selections?

- How well did children understand the skills presented in this theme? Which skills should be reviewed and practiced in the next theme?

- Did children enjoy the cooperative activities related to the major theme concept?

Formal Assessment

Select formal tests that meet your classroom needs:

- *Kindergarten Literacy Survey*

- Theme Skills Test for "Let's Be Friends"

See the *Teacher's Assessment Handbook* for guidelines for administering tests and using answer keys and children's sample papers.

Portfolio Assessment

Using Portfolios to Communicate with Parents During Conferences

Portfolios will help you demonstrate to parents the growth their children are making. Because portfolios are so interesting, you will need to plan carefully to make the best use of limited conference time. Send a note home before the conference telling what you hope the meeting will achieve. Allow ten minutes before the meeting for parents to look over their child's portfolio.

From the portfolio, select a few pieces of work from the start of the year and some current pieces. Use these to show parents their child's progress over time. As you discuss the work, explain your goals for the child.

Explain to parents how temporary spelling shows the child's progress in phonics and how it is an important stage in writing development.

Share what you plan to work on in the next few weeks or months.

For more information on this and other topics, see the *Teacher's Assessment Handbook.*

Celebrating the Theme

Choices for Celebrating

Celebrating the Theme:
Fold-Out Book About Friends

Make sure each child has written, or dictated, a sentence for their drawings for the class Fold-Out book. Then follow these steps to compile the book:

- Arrange the drawings side by side in a horizontal row.

- Tape the sides of the paper together.

- Fold the book up accordion-style and attach a cover made from tag board. Print the title *Friends At Home and At School* on the cover.

To celebrate the theme, display the class Fold-Out book. Have volunteers point out their contributions, read aloud what they wrote, and tell something about their drawing and writing.

Encourage children to share their thoughts and feelings about the theme celebration. Praise their contributions.

Internet See the Houghton Mifflin Internet resources for additional theme-related activities.

Self-Assessment

Have children meet in small groups to talk about what they learned in the theme. Use the following prompts to foster their discussion:

- What have you learned about friends in this theme?

- What did you learn that can help you become a better reader?

Book Talk

Display the covers of the theme books, asking children to recall the stories and their characters. Prompt additional discussion of the selections by asking:

- Do you think each story belongs in a theme called *Let's Be Friends*? Why or why not?

- Which story did you enjoy most? Why?

- What other books might you choose for a Let's Be Friends theme? Why?

Materials
- *Jamaica's Find*
- *What Shall We Do When We All Go Out?*
- *Together*

Theme Talk

Invite children to share what they've learned during the theme.

- Ask children to tell how learning about new words and sounds will help them to become better readers.

- Invite children to talk about the theme songs and poems and the books from the Reading and Listening Center they've enjoyed. Ask how the songs, poems, and books helped them learn more about being friends.

- Encourage children to share their favorite writing projects and activities.

Playful Pets

Table of Contents
THEME: Playful Pets

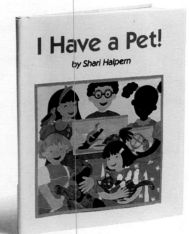
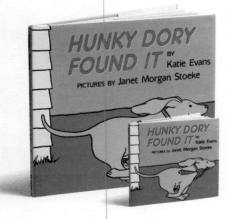

Bibliography

Books for the Library Corner

 Multicultural

 Science/Health

 Math

 Social Studies

 Music

 Art

My Dog
by Heidi Goennel
Orchard 1989 (32p)
A girl describes all the dogs she likes, but she likes her own dog best of all.

Bookstore Cat
by Cindy Wheeler
Random 1994 (32p) paper
Mulligan the cat has his paws full when two birds come into the bookstore where he works.

Let's Get a Puppy
by Caroline Ness
Harper 1994 (16p)
A boy shows his family that he can choose his own puppy.

Carl's Afternoon in the Park
by Alexandra Day
Farrar 1992 (32p)
Carl, a dog, baby-sits for a puppy and a toddler. **Available in Spanish as *Carlito en el parque una tarde.*** (Wordless)

Tabby
by Aliki
Harper 1995 (32p)
Graphic story of a kitten's first year with his young companion. (Wordless)

My Dog Rosie
by Isabelle Harper
Blue Sky 1994 (32p)
A young girl helps take care of her grandfather's dog.

If I Had a Pig
by Mick Inkpen
Dell (32p) 1992 paper
A boy imagines what it would be like to have a pet pig.

My Puppy
 by Inez Greene
Goodyear 1994 (8p)
A girl describes her playful new puppy. **Available in Spanish as *Mi perrito.***

The Great Cat Chase
by Mercer Mayer
Rain Bird Productions 1994 (32p) paper
Two children try to capture their escaped cat. (Wordless)

Our Dog
by Helen Oxenbury
Puffin 1992 (24p) paper
A boy and his mother walk their playful dog. **Available in Spanish as *Nuestro perro.***

Wake Up, Mr. B!
by Penny Dale
Candlewick 1992 (24p) also paper
Rosie's dog shares her early morning imaginations.

Toby the Tabby Kitten
 by Colleen Stanley Bare
Cobblehill 1995 (32p)
Photographs show Toby, a manx cat, growing from a kitten to an adult cat.

Where Is Jake?
by Mary Packard
Childrens 1990 (28p)
Two children search for their dog, who is always one step ahead of them. **Available in Spanish as *¿Dónde está Jake?***

Books for Teacher Read Aloud

Anteater on the Stairs
by Peter Cottrill
Kingfisher 1994 (24p)
Sophie's neighbor brags about his pets until he meets Sophie's polar bear.

So Many Cats!
by Beatrice Schenk de Regniers
 Clarion 1985 (32p) paper
One sad, lonely cat turns into twelve in this counting story.

Pet Show!
 by Ezra Jack Keats
Macmillan 1974 (40p) also paper
Archie almost misses the pet show when he can't find his cat.

The Hog Call to End All
by SuAnn Kiser
Orchard 1994 (32p)
Minerva hopes her pet hog will help her win a blue ribbon at the county fair.

The Golden Cage
 by Alma Flor Ada
Santillana 1993 (14p)
A young boy saves his money to buy his grandmother a very special gift. **Available in Spanish as *La jaula dorada.***

Insects Are My Life
by Megan McDonald
Orchard 1995 (32)
Amanda's friends tease her because she loves bugs.

Raining Cats and Dogs
by Jane Yolen
Harcourt 1993 (32p)
Eighteen appealing poems about dogs and cats.

On My Horse
 by Eloise Greenfield
Harper 1995 (16p)
A boy pretends the horse he rides in the park is his own.

Poonam's Pets

by Andrew and Diana Davies
Viking 1990 (24p) paper
Shy Poonam surprises her class when she brings six lions to a pet assembly.

Pets

Aladdin 1991 (24p) paper
The characteristics of gerbils, rabbits, dogs, cats, and other pets are simply described.

Mouse in the House

by Patricia Baer
Holiday 1994 (32p)
A woman trying to get rid of a mouse discovers that the mouse makes the best pet of all.

The New Puppy

by Laurence Anholt
Artists and Writers Guild Books 1994 (32p)
Anna learns that her new puppy requires much work and love.

My Cats Nick & Nora

by Isabelle Harper and Barry Moser
Scholastic 1995 (32p)
Isabelle and her cousin Emmie plan a festive birthday party for the cats Nick and Nora.

Books for Shared Reading

Dog Tales

by Janet McLean
Ticknor 1995 (32p)
Rhyming story of five dogs' daily spirited activities.

Have You Seen My Cat?

by Eric Carle
Scholastic 1991 (32p) paper
A boy searching for his missing cat finds a surprise.

City Dog

by Karla Kuskin
Clarion 1994 (32p)
A dog from the city has a hard time getting used to the country.

Dog In, Cat Out

by Gillian Rubinstein
Ticknor 1993 (32p)
A busy family's dog and cat take turns going in and out of the house.

Mary Had a Little Lamb

by Sarah Josepha Hale
Orchard 1995 (32p)
Fabric relief illustrations accompany the familiar nursery rhyme.

My Cat Jack

by Patricia Casey
Candlewick 1994 (32p)
A simple description of how a cat plays.

Hunky Dory Ate It

by Katie Evans
Dutton 1992 (32p)
After mischievous puppy Hunky Dory eats everything in sight, he has to be taken to the vet.

Emma's Pet

by David McPhail
Dutton 1985 (24p) also paper
Emma's search for a soft and cuddly pet leads her to her own father.

Splash

by Ann Jonas
Greenwillow 1995 (24p)
A girl's pets jump in and out of a pond while the reader calculates how many animals are in the water.

When the Fly Flew In...

by Lisa Westberg Peters
Dial 1994 (32p)
A child doesn't want to wake up his pets by cleaning his room, but a fly inadvertently gets the job done.

Technology Resources

Computer Software

Internet See the Houghton Mifflin Internet resources for additional bibliographic entries and theme-related activities.

Video Cassettes

Jim's Dog, Muffins by Miriam Cohen. Spoken Arts

Pet Show by Ezra Jack Keats. Weston Woods

To Bathe a Boa by C. Imbior Kudrna. Spoken Arts

Audio Cassettes

Mary Had a Little Lamb by Sara Josepha Hale. Am. Sch. Pub.

The Dog Who Had Kittens by Polly M. Robertus. Live Oak Media

Momo's Kitten by Mitsu and Taro Yashima. Am. Sch. Pub.

Whistle for Willie by Ezra Jack Keats. Am. Sch. Pub.

Filmstrips

Harry the Dirty Dog by Gene Zion. Am. Sch. Pub.

Emma's Pet by David McPhail. Live Oak Media

Old Mother Hubbard and Her Dog by Evaline Ness. Live Oak Media

AV addresses are in the Teacher's Handbook, pages H14–H15.

Theme at a Glance

Reading/Listening Center

Selections	Comprehension Skills and Strategies	Phonemic Awareness	Phonics/Decoding	Concepts About Print
I Have a Pet	✓ Compare/contrast, T121 Comparing and contrasting pet owners, T126 Finding likenesses and differences in animals, T126 Comparing pets, T126 Reading strategies, T116, T118, T120, T122 **Rereading and responding**, T124–T125	✓ Recognizes last sounds of spoken words, T117 Identifying last sounds in animal names, T127 Identify rhyming words, T127 Identifying same last sounds in words, T127		
Hunky Dory Found It	✓ Cause/effect, T149 Why things happen, T154 Causes of sound effects, T154 Identifying cause/effect relationships, T154 Reading strategies, T136, T138, T142, T144, T146, T148, T150 **Rereading and responding**, T152–T153		✓ Phonogram -it, T139 Initial p, T143 ✓ Initial k, T147 Decoding k words, T155 Finding words beginning with /k/, T155 Naming initial letters in spoken words, T155 Forming words with -it, T156 Reading words with -it, T156	✓ End of a written word, T141 Identifying the ends of words, T157 Naming the last letter in words, T157 Using spaces between words, T157
Snow on Snow on Snow	✓ Sequence of events, T181 Sequence of events in a story, T186 Recalling what happened first, T186 Identifying words that show order, T186 Reading strategies, T168, T170, T172, T174, T176, T180, T182 **Rereading and responding**, T184–T185		Initial f, T169 ✓ Initial c, T177 Decoding c words, T187 Finding pictures whose names begin with /k/, T187 Creating a collage with pictures whose names begin with /k/, T187 Reviewing initial consonant sounds, T188 Finding pictures whose names begin with /k/, T188 Naming foods whose names begin with /k/, T188	✓ Distinguishes the end of a line of text on left-hand and right-hand pages, T173 Reading sentences from left to right, T189 Identifying last line of type on pages, T189 Identifying ends of text lines, T189

✓ *Indicates Tested Skills.* See page T109 for assessment options.

Writing/Language Center

Cross-Curricular Center

Vocabulary	Listening	Oral Language	Writing	Content Areas
		Using describing words, T128 Making introductions, T128 Giving a persuasive talk, T128	Writing a book about a pet, T129 Creating prize ribbons for a pet show, T129 Listing supplies needed for a pet, T129	**Math:** creating a favorite-pets graph, T130 **Social Studies:** locating origins of pets, T130 **Science:** comparing animals' body coverings, T131 **Art:** creating cat masks, T131
✓ High-frequency word *it*, T137 Reading the high-frequency word *it*, T158 Using *it* in sentences, T158 Writing *it* in sentences, T158	Pantomiming instructions, T159 Listening for rhyming words, T159 Listening to *Hunky Dory Found It*, T159	Dramatizing events at the vet's office, T160 Using sense words to describe items, T160 Using describing words, T160	Class story, T135 Writing a description, T161 Writing about mischievous pets, T161 Creating lost-and-found posters, T161	**Social Studies:** learning about working animals, T162 **Math:** making, recording, and comparing estimates, T162 **Art:** responding to master paintings that include pets, T163 **Science:** learning about the helpful effects of wind, T163; learning how to care for pets, T163
✓ High-frequency word *did*, T175 Reading *did* in sentences, T190 Reading high-frequency words, T190 Reading and forming sentences with *did* and *it*, T190 Reading a story with *did* and *it*, T190	Listening for information, T191 Listening to *Snow on Snow on Snow*, T191 Asking and responding to questions, T191	Describing how to care for pets, T194 Describing what people do in winter and summer, T194 Sharing songs and poems about pets, T194 Using order words, T194	Class story, T167 Writing words that name and describe pets, T193 Writing reactions to stories, T193 Completing health records for pets, T195 Writing sentences about pets, T195 Writing lost pet notices, T195	**Math:** making pet licenses from cookie dough, T196 **Social Studies:** making compasses, T196 **Music:** singing songs and creating song variations, T197 **Art:** finger painting with soap flakes, T197

Meeting Individual Needs

Key to Meeting Individual Needs

 Students Acquiring English

Activities and notes throughout the lesson plans offer strategies to help children understand the selections and lessons.

 Challenge

Challenge activities and notes throughout the lesson plans suggest additional activities to stimulate critical and creative thinking.

 Extra Support

Activities and notes throughout the lesson plans offer additional strategies to help children experience success.

Managing Instruction

Cooperative Groups

Young children must be taught how to work cooperatively. Begin with partner work during whole class activities. Show partners how to take turns and share materials. Move next to triads with activities that have three parts, such as telling a story with a beginning, middle and end. In triads, develop skills for active listening and turn-taking. Gradually work up to groups of four.

For further information on this and other Managing Instruction topics, see the *Professional Development Handbook*.

Performance Standards

During this theme, children will

- *share in the joys of having real or imaginary pets*
- *monitor their reading and ask self-questions*
- *retell or summarize each selection*
- *apply comprehension skills: Compare and Contrast; Cause and Effect; Sequence*
- *recognize the last sounds of spoken words and the end of a written line*
- *recognize words beginning with* k *and* c *and words containing the phonogram* -it
- *recognize the high-frequency words* it *and* did
- *write a story*

Students Acquiring English	Challenge	Extra Support
• **Develop Key Concepts** Children focus on Key Concepts through dramatizing and making charts to organize story concepts.	• **Apply Critical Thinking** Children apply critical thinking by comparing and contrasting, recognizing cause and effect relationships, and placing events in the correct sequence.	• **Enhance Self-Confidence** With extra support provided for reading and responding to the literature, children will see themselves as active members of the reading community.
• **Expand Vocabulary** Throughout the theme, children use context and picture clues, discuss meanings, and model definitions. Children expand their vocabulary to include multiple-meaning words, pronoun referents, and position words.	• **Explore Topics of Interest** Activities that motivate further exploration include classifying pets, learning about guide dogs, and making a compass.	• **Receive Increased Instructional Time on Skills** Practice activities in the Reading/Listening Center provide support with comparing and contrasting, cause and effect, and sequence.
• **Act as a Resource** Children are asked to share their experiences with different kinds of pets and their knowledge of various breakfast foods eaten around the world.	• **Engage in Creative Thinking** Opportunities for creative expression include making a pet shopping list, creating cat masks, making prize ribbons, taking an imaginary trip, and writing about the perfect pet.	• **Provide Independent Reading** Children can also take home the Tear-and-Take stories in their *Literacy Activity Books* and the black-and-white versions of the WATCH ME READ titles to read.

Additional Resources

Invitaciones

Develop bi-literacy with this integrated reading/language arts program in Spanish. Provides authentic literature and real-world resources from Spanish-speaking cultures.

Language Support

Translations of Big Books in Chinese, Hmong, Khmer, and Vietnamese. *Teacher's Booklet* provides instructional support in English.

Students Acquiring English Handbook

Guidelines, strategies, and additional instruction for students acquiring English.

Planning for Assessment

Informal Assessment

Observation Checklist

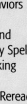

- Concepts About Print/Book Handling
- Responding to Literature and Decoding Behaviors and Strategies
- Writing Behaviors and Stages of Temporary Spelling
- Listening and Speaking Behaviors
- Story Retelling and Rereading

Literacy Activity Book

Recommended pages for students' portfolios:
- Personal Response, p. 123
- Comprehension: Cause and Effect, p. 125
- Language Patterns, p. 131
- Phonics/Decoding: Letter *c*, p. 133

Retellings—Oral/Written

- *Teacher's Assessment Handbook*

Formal Assessment

Kindergarten Literacy Survey

Evaluates children's literacy development. Provides holistic indicator of children's ability with
- Shared Reading/Constructing Meaning
- Concepts About Print
- Phonemic Awareness
- Emergent Writing

Kindergarten Literacy Survey

Integrated Theme Test

- General Comprehension
- Letter Sounds *k* and *c*
- Phonogram *-it*
- Writing

Integrated Theme Test

Theme Skills Test

- Cause and Effect
- Recognizes Last Sounds of Spoken Words
- Letter Sounds *k* and *c*
- High-Frequency Words *it* and *did*
- Phonogram *-it*

Theme Skills Test

Managing Assessment

Monitoring Independent Work

Question: How can I monitor children's independent reading and writing?

Answer: Even in kindergarten children should spend time in independent reading and writing. Try these tips for keeping track:

- For monitoring reading, use a book log that includes a place for children to copy, or for them to dictate to you, the names of their books. Provide a place for them to show how well they liked the book using happy/sad faces or pictures.

- Provide time for children to share the books they like (read aloud, shared reading, or independent reading). Encourage children to talk about and draw about favorites.

- Use children's journals to monitor independent writing. Drawings are often the beginnings of writing for young children. Encourage them to share their drawings/writing.

- Focus on a few children each time you have independent reading and writing. Notice children who are able to stick with their reading and writing and those who need extra support.

For more information on this and other topics, see the *Teacher's Assessment Handbook*.

Portfolio Assessment

The portfolio icon signals portfolio opportunities throughout the theme.

Additional Portfolio Tips:
- Evaluating Work in the Portfolio, T199

Launching the Theme

 See the Houghton Mifflin **Internet** resources for additional activities.

Song Tape for Playful Pets: *"Mary Had a Little Lamb"*

INTERACTIVE LEARNING

Warm-up

Singing the Theme Song

- Play the tape. Invite children who know the song to sing along. (See lyrics in the Teacher's Handbook, page H13.)

- Discuss what might happen if children brought a lamb to school.

- Play the song again, and encourage children to sing along.

Interactive Bulletin Board

All Kinds of Pets Invite children to share pets they have or would like to have with the class. Children might:

- Bring in photographs of their own pets.

- Find and clip from magazines pictures of real pets they'd like to have.

- Draw pictures of imaginary pets.

Talk about the responsibilities involved in owning a pet. Note with children that all pets need proper care, but that some need more attention than others.

Ongoing Project

A Class Pet

Invite children to learn about and care for a class pet or a pet the class would like to have. You may wish to follow these steps with children:

- Brainstorm a list of animals that would make good class pets. Discuss why fish or gerbils are good choices for a classroom while dogs or cats are not. Decide which pet would be best for your classroom.

- Create a Pet Corner to house the class pet, its cage or tank, a supply of food, and books and pictures about it.

- List jobs that need to be done to care for the pet on a "Taking Care of Our Pet" chart. Rotate jobs so all children share the care of the pet.

 See the *Home/Community Connections Booklet* for theme-related materials.

Portfolio Opportunity

The Portfolio Opportunity icon highlights portfolio opportunities throughout the theme.

Choices for Centers

Creating Centers

Use these activities to create learning centers in the classroom.

Reading/Listening Center

- Picture Card Pets, T126
- Sound Effects, T154
- "C" Word Collage, T187

Language/Writing Center

- Let's Have a Pet Show, T129
- Dramatic Play: At the Vet's, T160
- Writing Notices, T195

Cross-Curricular Center

- Math: Favorite Pets Graph, T130
- Social Studies: Working Dogs, T162
- Art: Painting with "Snow," T197

READ ALOUD

SELECTION:

I Have a Pet!

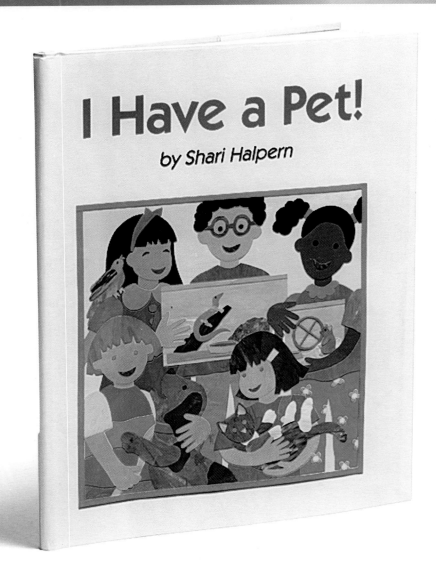

by Shari Halpern

Other Books by the Author

My River

Moving from One to Ten

What Shall We Do When We All Go Out?

Selection Summary

A pet show provides five children with an opportunity to share details about the habits and care of their pets: a dog, a cat, a parakeet, a hamster, and a lizard. As the young owners wait in line to present their pets to the judge, the animals succumb to their instincts, at one point causing complete chaos. And which pet will the judge choose as best in show? With a stroke of genius, he makes everyone a winner, with prizes awarded for "Best Tricks," "Softest Fur," "Best Song," "Best Purr," and "Most Unusual."

Lesson Planning Guide

	Skill/Strategy Instruction	Meeting Individual Needs	Lesson Resources
1 Introduce *the* Literature *Pacing: 1 day*	**Preparing to Listen and Write** Warm-up/Build Background, T112 Read Aloud, T112	**Choices for Rereading,** T115 **Students Acquiring English,** T115	**Poster** My Bird Is Small, T114 *Literacy Activity Book* Personal Response, p. 119
2 Interact *with* Literature *Pacing: 1-2 days*	**Reading Strategies** Monitor, T116, T118 Self-Question, T116, T118 Evaluate, T118, T122 Summarize, T120 **Minilessons** ✔ Recognizes Last Sounds of Spoken Words, T117 ✔ Compare and Contrast, T121	**Extra Support,** T117 **Students Acquiring English,** T118 **Challenge,** T119, T120 **Rereading and Responding,** T124-T125	**Story Props,** T125, H4 See the Houghton Mifflin **Internet** resources for additional activities.
3 Instruct *and* Integrate *Pacing: 1-2 days*	**Reading/Listening Center,** Comprehension, T126 Phonemic Awareness, T127 **Language/Writing Center,** Oral Language, T128 Writing, T129 **Cross-Curricular Center,** Cross-Curricular Activities, T130-T131	**Challenge,** T127, T129 **Extra Support,** T127, T128 **Students Acquiring English,** T126, T128, T130	**Posters** My Bird Is Small, T127 Class Pet Care, T129 *Literacy Activity Book* Comprehension, p. 121 **Letter, Picture, and Word Cards,** T127 See the Houghton Mifflin **Internet** resources for additional activities.

✔ *Indicates Tested Skills. See page T109 for assessment options.*

Introduce *the* Literature

Preparing to Listen and Write

Poster

My bird is small.
My bird is shy.
It does not sing.
It cannot fly.
It does no tricks
and that is fine.

I love my bird.
My bird is mine.

KARLA KUSKIN

My Bird Is Small

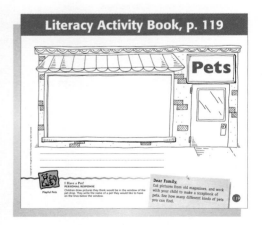

Literacy Activity Book, p. 119

INTERACTIVE LEARNING

Warm-up/Build Background

Sharing a Poem

- Read aloud the poem "My Bird Is Small."

- Discuss the poem with children. Ask if children agree that a child can love a pet, even if it doesn't do anything special. Invite children to share pets they have, or know, and love.

- Invite children to read the poem along with you. They might chime in on the word *bird*, as well as on the rhyming words.

Read Aloud

LAB, p. 119

Preview and Predict

- Display the cover of *I Have a Pet!* Explain that Shari Halpern wrote the words and created the art for the story.

- Discuss the cover illustration with children. Ask if children have pets like the ones pictured here.

- Take a picture walk through the story, inviting children to tell what they think is happening. Encourage children to:

  –identify the pets on pages 4-5, and tell who they think the man is;

  –name the pet pictured on page 7, and predict what the dog's owner might be saying about his pet on pages 8-9;

  –note that each child in turn tells about his or her pet, with a brief interruption on pages 18-19, when the bird causes some confusion;

  –predict why everyone looks so unhappy on pages 28-29;

  –tell what the happy ending to the story is.

Read

Read the story aloud for children, sharing the pictures as you do so and inviting additional responses to them. Talk with children about how their predictions about the story did or did not match what actually happened.

Personal Response

Home Connection Have children complete *Literacy Activity Book* page 119 to show which pet they would like to have. Invite children to take the page home and retell the story to their families.

Appreciating the Artist's Craft

Display pages 4-5, and ask if children can figure out how Shari Halpern created the people and the pets on this page. Explain that each shape—hair, eyes, mouth, shirtsleeve, dog's ear—was cut from a piece of paper that Shari Halpern had painted. Then all the shapes were pasted onto a sheet of white paper.

Ask which of the pet owners on pages 4-5 children think was hardest to make. Which pet was the hardest? Have children look at the pictures as you reread the story. Encourage them to note details that show the artist's craft, such as the bee on the flower on page 8 and all the bits of wood chips in the hamster's cage on page 22.

Pantomiming Characters' Actions

To help children identify with story characters, ask volunteers to pantomime the actions of the five pet owners as you reread the story. Invite a new volunteer to step forward to perform after each page with the sentence "I have a pet!"

Students Acquiring English You might want to pair up children who are learning English with native speakers to try this activity together.

Drawing Conclusions

Display the illustration on page 5, and have children note both the clipboard and the pencil in the judge's pocket. Explain that as you reread the story, you'd like volunteers to tell what the judge might be writing about each pet. Pause after those pages on which pet owners describe their pets; hand various children a clipboard and ask what they think the judge might write.

More Choices for Rereading

Rereadings provide varied, repeated experiences with the literature so that children can make its language and content their own. The following rereading choices appear on page T124.

- Interpreting Characters' Feelings
- Sequencing of Events
- Noting Details to Create a Fantasy Pet

Interact *with* Literature

READ ALOUD

Reading Strategies

▶ **Monitor/Self-Question**

Teacher Modeling Mention that if children were reading this book on their own, they'd probably need to stop fairly often to ask themselves:

- Does this make sense?
- Did I miss something?

Model for children how you might apply strategic reading to pages 4-9 of the story.

Think Aloud

There are no words on pages 4-5 of the story. That's unusual. I see several children with pets. I'm not sure who the man is. I think I should read on to see if things become clear. I see the same children on pages 6-7. One child, a boy with a dog, is going up to the man. I think he is the one saying "I have a pet!" On pages 8-9, I see a lot of words. I think the boy is telling the man about his pet dog on these pages.

Note that the art on pages 8-9 looks a little different, too. Each picture is in a box and shows a "close-up" of the child and the dog from page 7.

Purpose Setting

Invite children to listen as you read the story again. Ask them to think about who is telling about a pet— and what that pet is.

I have a pet!

6

7

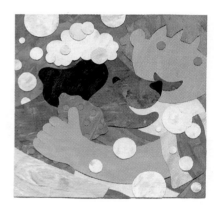

My dog's name is Bucky. I take him out for his walks. He is curious and likes to sniff everything. Bucky is also smart. I taught him to sit and to give me his paw.

8

I give Bucky a bath when he is dirty. It is a big job, and sometimes Bucky doesn't cooperate. But when his bath is done, he smells nice and clean. I love my dog.

9

Quick**REFERENCE**

Science Link

Ask which pets are in carrying cases or cages, and why. Help children find the water and/or food containers in the hamster, bird, and lizard cages. Discuss that animals, like people, need both food and water to survive.

Vocabulary

Ask how Bucky shows that he is curious. (He sniffs everything.) Ask if children think most dogs are curious. Also discuss the meaning of *cooperate*. Ask why a dog might not want to cooperate when it's time for a bath.

Phonemic Awareness Review

Say the words *dog* and *Bucky*. Ask children to identify the first sound in each word. (/d/ in *dog*; /b/ in *Bucky*)

I have a pet!

10

11

This is my cat, Fern. I help take Fern to the vet so she can get her vaccinations. They keep her healthy. Every year we make sure Fern goes for shots.

12

My favorite time with Fern is at night when I'm about to go to sleep. She curls up in a little ball near my pillow, and I can hear her purring. That means she's happy. I love my cat.

13

High-Frequency Words

Display page 11. On the chalkboard, write *I have a pet!* Ask volunteers to take turns reading the sentence.

Extra Support

Concept Development Explain that vaccinations are given to people and to animals to prevent them from catching certain diseases. Ask if children recall getting vaccinations for diseases such as polio or measles.

 Multicultural Link

Different cultures view animals in different ways and often keep different kinds of animals as pets. In Japan, mice are among the favorite pets of children. These mice are often tamed and taught to "dance" to music.

Phonemic Awareness

Recognizes Last Sounds of Spoken Words

TESTED SKILL

Teach/Model

Remind children that Fern is a pet cat, and that Fern goes to the vet to get shots. Ask children to listen for the *first* sound in *pet* as you say the word. Say *pet;* then say /p/ with children. Ask them to listen for the *last* sounds. Say *pet* again; then say /et/ with children.

Repeat with the words *cat* and *vet.* For *vet,* encourage children to say the last sounds—/et/—by themselves.

Practice/Apply

Ask children to listen as you say several words. Say each of these words, followed by the question:

- **dog** What are the last sounds, /d/ or /og/?
- **sit** What are the last sounds, /s/ or /it/?
- **bath** What are the last sounds, /b/ or /ath/?

SKILL FINDER

Last Sounds in Animal Names, page T127

Interact *with* Literature

Reading Strategies

 Evaluate

Teacher Modeling Ask if Bucky the dog and Fern the cat are like the dogs and cats children know.

Think Aloud

I know lots of dogs that don't like baths. So I think what the boy says about Bucky not liking baths makes sense. I agree with what he says. I agree with what Fern's owner says, too. Cats, like dogs, need to get vaccinations so they stay healthy. And some cats do curl up with their owners when they go to sleep.

 Monitor/Self-Question

Teacher Modeling Ask if children wondered, at first, why everyone looks so upset in the picture on pages 18-19.

Think Aloud

When I look at the pictures on pages 18-19, I see that the bird flies up into the air when its owner takes it out of the cage. I think this makes the other animals, and their owners, excited.

Help children note that the animals seem calmer when George, the parakeet, is back with its owner.

I have a pet!

14

15

My pet is a bird, and his name is George. He is a parakeet. I give George birdseed and water, and I change the paper at the bottom of his cage when it gets dirty.

16

George sings. Sometimes he chirps softly, and other times he squawks loudly. Sometimes he stands on my shoulder and sings to me. I love my bird.

17

 **Quick REFERENCE**

Students Acquiring English

Use the illustrations to help children who are learning English to understand the words *parakeet*, *birdseed*, and *shoulder*.

18

19

20

I have a pet!

21

Read Aloud pp. 18-21

QuickREFERENCE

Journal

The children in this story end their descriptions by saying that they love their pets. Children might draw and write in their journals about animals they love.

MEETING INDIVIDUAL NEEDS

Challenge

Antonyms Review that sometimes George chirps softly and squawks loudly. Explain that *softly* and *loudly* are opposite in meaning. Ask children to say something softly and then loudly.

Vocabulary

Word Meanings Review that George *sings, chirps,* and *squawks*—just like most parakeets. Ask children to mimic these sounds.

Interact
with
Literature

Reading Strategies

▶ **Summarize**

Teacher Modeling Help children list the animals in *I Have a Pet!*

dog	hamster
cat	lizard
parakeet	

Show children how to use the list to tell what has happened up through page 27 of the story. Then invite children to use the list to summarize the story.

Sophie is my hamster. I give her food and water, and I clean out her cage. I take out the old, dirty wood chips and put in new, clean ones. Sophie likes to burrow under them and make a soft bed to sleep in.

22

I like to hold Sophie in my hands and watch her little pink nose wiggle up and down. She is so small and her fur is so smooth. I am very gentle with her. I love my hamster.

23

I have a pet!

24

25

QuickREFERENCE

Challenge

MEETING INDIVIDUAL NEEDS

Antonyms Review that Sophie's owner takes out old, dirty wood chips and puts in new, clean ones. Ask which word means the opposite of *old.* (new) Ask which word means the opposite of *dirty.* (clean)

This is my pet lizard. His name is Raymond. He lives in a glass cage with a rock and a branch that he likes to sit on. I make sure Raymond gets fresh water and crickets to eat.

26

I like to hold Raymond. He doesn't feel slimy. He feels dry and smooth. Sometimes Raymond sheds his skin. I think Raymond is an interesting pet. I love my lizard.

27

28

29

Background: FYI

There are over 3,000 different kinds of lizards. All lizards have dry, scaly skin and clawed toes. These cold-blooded reptiles usually live where it's warm; those that do live in cold climates hibernate during the winter.

Vocabulary

Ask children to name something that feels *slimy.* Then ask them to name something that feels *dry* and *smooth.* Discuss *sheds,* as in *sheds his skin.* Point out that as a lizard grows a new skin, it gets rid of, or sheds, its old skin.

Home Connection

Encourage children to talk about pets they may have at home with their families. Suggest that children find out what needs to be done to take care of the pet and to share this information with the class.

Comprehension:
Compare/
Contrast

TESTED SKILL

Teach/Model

Discuss how the children in this story are alike.

Think Aloud

Each child has a pet, and each one wants to win the contest. Each child tells how he or she takes care of the pet and ends by saying that he or she loves the pet. So the pet owners are alike in many ways.

Then display these sentences, and help children read them:

- I have a pet.
- I take care of my pet.
- I love my pet.

Lead children to see that any one of the children in the story could have said these sentences; they show how the children are alike.

Note that one way the children in the story are different is that they have different *kinds* of pets.

Practice/Apply

Arrange children in groups of five to role play the pet owners in the story. Have children take turns telling one way in which they are alike and one way in which they are different.

SKILL FINDER

Alike and Different, page T126

Minilessons, Themes 4 and 12

READ ALOUD

Reading Strategies

▶ **Evaluate**

Teacher Modeling Talk about the ending of the story with children. Discuss how the judge gives each pet a prize to surprise both the pet owners and the readers.

Think Aloud

I know that most pet shows, like other contests, have one winner. The ending of this story surprised me because each pet wins a prize. I think the judge is very clever to give a special prize to each pet.

Encourage children to share their impressions of the story.

30

31

Which pet would *you* like to have?

Self-Assessment

Have children ask themselves:

● Do I like this story? Can I tell someone why I do or do not like it?

QuickREFERENCE

Visual Literacy

Ask if children have ever seen prize ribbons like the ones in the picture on pages 30-31. Have children ever won such ribbons?

Journal

Ask each child to make a prize ribbon for the animal he or she has written about. Allow children to use temporary spellings for the words they wish to write on their ribbons.

Visual Literacy

Read the words on the pet shop with children. Ask what the sign on the door might say when the shop is *not* open. *(closed)* Ask why they think the word *new* appears above the turtle. Ask what they might write on a sign for the window.

Interact with Literature

Rereading

More Choices for Rereading

Interpreting Characters' Feelings

As you read the story, help children note how the expressions on the pet owners' faces change at various points. Encourage children to comment on how the characters might be feeling. You might use questions such as these:

- pages 6-7: Why do all the pet owners look happy? (They're excited about the pet contest.)

- pages 14-15: Why do all the pet owners look worried? (The bird is out of its cage; the cat and the dog look as if they'd like to get that bird.)

- pages 18-19: Why does everyone look upset? (The bird has flown up into the air; the dog is pulling at its leash; the cat is jumping on the judge.)

- pages 20-21: Everyone now seems calm. Why? (The bird is back with its owner.)

- pages 28-29: The judge looks puzzled, and the pet owners look unhappy. Why? (Everyone is thinking about who will get the prize.)

- pages 30-31: Now everyone is smiling. Why? (Each pet has won a prize.)

Sequencing of Events

To help children focus on the order in which things happen in this story, have them sit in a circle and take turns retelling it as you turn the pages of the Read-Aloud Book.

Noting Details to Create a Fantasy Pet

Challenge Read the story, noting with children each pet's special features. Then invite children to create new imaginary pets by combining two or more of these features. Encourage children to draw pictures of their imaginary pets, name them, and make up a story about them. Invite children to share their stories with the class.

Informal Assessment

Use Story Talk or the dramatization activity to assess children's general understanding of *I Have a Pet!*

Responding

Choices for Responding

Story Talk

Have children work in groups of two or three to discuss these questions:

- Are the pets in this story lucky to have the owners they do? Why or why not?

- What might have happened if George, the parakeet, had flown away?

- What would you tell the judge in the story about your pet—or about the class pet?

Personal Response

Ask which pet children would have chosen as "the very best," if they were the judge. Have them draw first-prize ribbons for those pets. Children can share their ideas and explain their choices.

Role-Playing Endings

Ask children what might have happened if each pet had not won a prize. Ask one group of children to act out the end of the story—as it actually happened. Ask another group to act out a new ending.

Dramatizing *I Have a Pet!*

Help children to make hand puppets for *I Have a Pet!* Then invite them to use the props to act out the story. Children playing pet owners should begin with the story line: "I have a pet!" They can then improvise on the dialogue as they tell about their pets.

Materials

- Story Retelling Props hand puppets (See Teacher's Handbook, page H4.)

Portfolio Opportunity

For a writing sample, save children's drawings from the Personal Response activity.

Instruct *and* Integrate

Comprehension

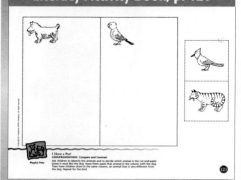
Practice Activities

Alike and Different

LAB, p. 121

Extra Support Review the many ways in which the pet owners are alike and different. Page through the story, helping children use word and picture clues to compare and contrast the owners. Next, ask children to tell how the story pets are alike and different. Use a chart to help organize their ideas.

Have children complete *Literacy Activity Book* page 121.

	dog	cat	bird	hamster	lizard
fur	✓	✓		✓	
feathers			✓		
scales					✓
4 legs	✓	✓		✓	✓
2 legs			✓		
wings			✓		
tail	✓	✓	✓	✓	✓

Picture Card Pets

Display all the Picture Cards that feature animals. Then arrange children in small groups. Have each group choose two or three pictures of animals that are alike in some way. They might choose, for example, farm animals, pets, animals with feathers, and so on.

Suggest that children then name at least two ways in which the animals are different. Have groups take turns showing the animals and telling classmates how they are alike and how they are different.

Comparing Pets

Invite children to compare the pets from the story with pets they or their neighbors have. Children might draw pictures of the animals and then dictate two sentences: one telling how the animals are alike and another telling how they are different.

Students Acquiring English Create a chart similar to the one in the Alike and Different activity. Children who are learning English benefit from this kind of visual representation and organization.

Informal Assessment

As children complete the activities on these pages

- note their ability to compare and contrast
- recognize the last sounds in spoken words.

Phonemic Awareness

Practice Activities

Last Sounds in Animal Names

Extra Support Assign each child a partner. Hold up a Picture Card, and ask children to listen carefully as you name it, for example *pig*. Then give the card to one pair of children. Ask one child which is the first sound; say both the first and last sounds so the child can choose between them. Ask the other child which are the last sounds; again, say both first and last sounds so the child can choose.

Materials
- Picture Cards: *bear, bird, cat, cow, deer, dog, fish, fox, goat, mouse, pig, seal, yak*

Rhyming Words— Last Sounds

Display the poster and read "My Bird Is Small" with children. Then point to and say the words *fine* and *mine*. Ask: What are the last sounds in *fine*: /f/ or /ine/? What are the last sounds in *mine*: /m/ or /ine/?

Note that *fine* and *mine* have the same last sounds, /ine/. Explain that when words have the same last sounds we say that they *rhyme*.

Challenge Encourage children to name other words that have the same last sounds as *fine* and *mine*. (*dine, line, pine, vine*)

Name the Animals

Challenge Provide partners with an animal Picture Card from the Last Sounds in Animal Names activity above. Have children say the animal name and identify the last sounds in the word. Then ask children to think of a name for the animal that has the same last sounds. Encourage children to share the names they choose with the class to verify that the last sounds are indeed the same.

Portfolio Opportunity

Save children's Comparing Pets drawings as a record of their ability to compare and contrast.

Oral Language

Choices for Oral Language

Describing Words

Display pages 30-31 and read aloud the words on the prize ribbons. Ask children to find the three ribbons that have the word *best*. (best tricks, best song, best purr) Explain that we use the word *best* when we compare several things. You might write the following on the chalkboard, and ask children to demonstrate:

- a good trick (or song or purr)
- a better trick
- the best trick

Next, ask children to name something in the class that feels soft. Then ask them to find something that is even softer. Finally, give children balls of cotton to feel, and ask if it is softest of all.

Invite children to suggest other words that might be used to describe one of the story pets.

Bucky, Meet Fern! Fern, Meet Bucky!

Have children practice making introductions by role playing the pet owners in the story and introducing their pets to one another. Review how to make an introduction. Encourage children to tell something about the pets as they introduce them.

Students Acquiring English You might pair up children who are learning English with native speakers to practice introducing first themselves, then one another, and finally their pets.

Giving a Persuasive Talk

Discuss with children how each pet owner in the story tried to persuade the judge that his or her pet should win the contest. Encourage children to give such talks about their own pets or those in the story. Or, each child could bring in a stuffed animal from home and tell why that animal should win a contest.

Extra Support Suggest that children practice their talks in small groups before presenting them to the entire class.

Informal Assessment

Observe children as they make their introductions or give their persuasive talks to note the fluency and clarity of their speech. Also observe whether children can successfully copy sentences and whether they try to sound out the initial consonants of words they want to use.

 # Writing

Choices for Writing

Let's Have a Pet Show

Remind children that each pet owner began telling about his or her pet by saying: "I have a pet!" After telling about the pet, each owner said, "I love my (kind of pet)."

Write the following on the chalkboard:

I have a pet!
I love my _____.

Show children how to fold drawing paper to make a four-page book. Then have them:

- Copy the first sentence onto the covers of their books and draw a picture to show a pet they'd like to have.

- Copy the last sentence onto the last page, naming the pet.

- Draw pictures to show how they'd care for the pet on the inside two pages.

Invite children to share their books. Award each child a prize ribbon cut from blue construction paper for his or her efforts.

Prize Ribbons for Pets

Challenge Invite children to make prize ribbons for pets they have or would like to have. Children might like to make prize ribbons for the animals they wrote about for Let's Have a Pet Show. Encourage children to use describing words on their prize labels.

Pet Care

Talk briefly with children about things someone would need to take care of a pet. Have them work in small groups to make lists of things.

Invite children to share their lists. Guide them in comparing their lists to things shown in the poster "Class Pet Care."

> **Materials**
> - "Class Pet Care" Poster

Poster

CLASS PET CARE

brush · scale · shampoo · vegetables · food bowl · fruit

Portfolio Opportunity

For a writing sample, save children's prize ribbons or their books from Let's Have a Pet Show.

Cross-Curricular Activities

Math

Favorite Pets Graph

Recall with children the different pets in *I Have a Pet!* Then begin a discussion of favorite pets, listing the animals on the chalkboard as they are suggested.

- Help children construct a graph with the pet names as headings.

- Ask each child to tell which pet is his or her favorite, using a check mark to record the vote on the graph.

- Have children decide—without counting—which pets are most popular. Have them confirm their responses by stacking interlocking plastic math cubes for each pet.

- Invite children to draw pictures to illustrate the headings.

Favorite Pets

Cat	Dog	Bird
✓	✓	✓
✓	✓	
	✓	

Social Studies

Pets Around the World

Materials
- pictures of various breeds of cats
- world map

★★★ **Multicultural Link** Ask children to describe their own pet cats or those of neighbors. Explain that cats are popular pets all around the world, and that different kinds of cats come from different countries. Display photographs of several domestic cat breeds and show on a map or globe where each is from. For example:

- Manx—from Great Britain

- Siamese cats—from Thailand

- Russian blues—from Russia

Students Acquiring English Invite children who are learning English to tell about special cats from their native countries.

Science

Fur, Feathers, Scales, or Smooth

Explain that people who study animals group them in special ways by finding how the animals are alike. Tell children that one way they do this is by looking at an animal's body covering. Pass around the fur, feathers, and fish (lizard) to help children name body coverings animals might have. Then make a chart with the headings Fur, Feathers, Scales, and Smooth. Discuss the headings with children to categorize the animals in *I Have a Pet!*

Invite children to add other animals to the chart. Display the pictures you've gathered one at a time, asking children to share what they know about that animal. Have a volunteer tape the picture under the appropriate heading.

Materials
- piece of furry fabric
- feathers
- plastic fish or lizard with scales
- pictures of mammals, birds, fish, reptiles, and amphibians

Animal Groups

fur	feathers	scales	smooth
dog	parakeet	lizard	(frog)
cat	(hen)	(fish)	(toad)
hamster	(duck)	(snake)	(salamander)

Art

Cat Masks

Invite children to make cat masks or masks for other story animals.

1. Cut holes in paper plates for children's eyes and noses.

2. Have children decorate the masks by drawing stripes or spots for fur and pasting on thin strips of paper for whiskers.

3. Attach a craft stick to the base of each mask as a handle.

4. Have children hold the masks before their faces and pretend to be cats.

Materials
- paper plates
- construction paper
- craft sticks
- glue

BIG BOOK

SELECTION:

Hunky Dory Found It

by Katie Evans

Other Books by Katie Evans

Hunky Dory Ate It

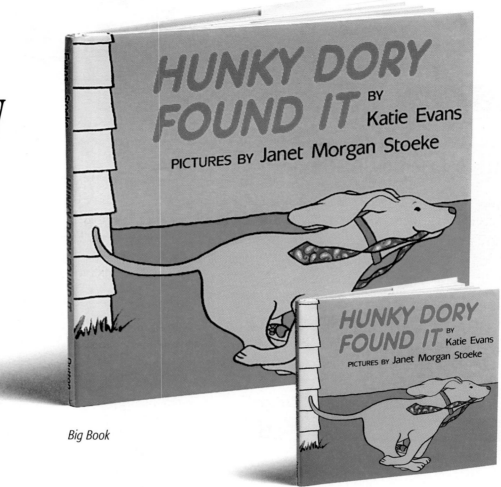

Big Book

Little Big Book

Selection Summary

Hunky Dory has an incurable habit: he can't resist running off with people's things. He snatches Sarah Locke's sock and Tommy Hall's ball. He even takes Baby Sue's shoe. His collection of treasures grows and grows—until his owner discovers it. Then back to the rightful owners everything must go. Maybe.

Lesson Planning Guide

	Skill/Strategy Instruction	Meeting Individual Needs	Lesson Resources
1 Introduce *the* Literature *Pacing: 1 day*	**Shared Reading and Writing** Warm-up/Build Background, T134 Shared Reading, T134 Shared Writing, T135	Choices for Rereading, T135 Students Acquiring English, T135	**Poster** In Downtown Philadelphia, T134 *Literacy Activity Book* Personal Response, p. 123
2 Interact *with* Literature *Pacing: 1–2 days*	**Reading Strategies** Self-Question, T136 Monitor, T136, T144, T146 Think About Words, T138 Summarize, T142 Evaluate, T142, T148, T150 Predict/Infer, T150 **Minilessons** ✔ High-Frequency Words: *it*, T137 ✔ Phonogram -*it*, T139 ✔ End of a Written Word, T141 Initial *p*, T143 ✔ Initial *k,* T147 ✔ Cause and Effect, T149	Students Acquiring English, T138, T140, T147, T149, T152 Extra Support, T137, T148 Challenge, T143 Rereading and Responding, T152-T153	**Story Props,** T15, H4 **Letter, Word, and Picture Cards,** T137, T139, T147 *Literacy Activity Book* Language Patterns, p. 124 See the Houghton Mifflin **Internet** resources for additional activities.
3 Instruct *and* Integrate *Pacing: 1–2 days*	**Reading/Listening Center** Comprehension, T154 Phonics/Decoding, T155-T156 Concepts About Print, T157 Vocabulary, T158 Listening, T159 **Language/Writing Center** Oral Language, T160 Writing, T161 **Cross-Curricular Center** Cross-Curricular Activities, T162-T163	Challenge, T156, T161, T162 Extra Support, T154, T155, T156, T157, T158, T161	**Poster** In Downtown Philadelphia, T157 **Letter, Word, and Picture Cards,** T155, T156, T158 **My Big Dictionary,** T155 *Literacy Activity Book* Comprehension, p. 125 Phonics/Decoding, pp. 127-128 Vocabulary, p. 129 **Audio Tape** for Playful Pets: *Hunky Dory Found It* See the Houghton Mifflin **Internet** resources for additional activities.

✔ *Indicates Tested Skills. See page T109 for assessment options.*

1 Introduce *the* Literature

Shared Reading and Writing

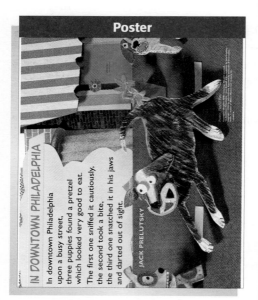

Poster

IN DOWNTOWN PHILADELPHIA

In downtown Philadelphia
upon a busy street,
three puppies found a pretzel
which looked very good to eat.
The first one sniffed it cautiously,
the second took a bite,
the third one snatched it in his jaws
and darted out of sight.

JACK PRELUTSKY

INTERACTIVE LEARNING

Warm-up/Build Background

Sharing a Poem
- Invite children to follow along as you read the poem "In Downtown Philadelphia."

- Ask if children have ever seen puppies behaving this way. Encourage them to think about dogs they know. What would these dogs do, sniff the pretzel cautiously or snatch it and run away?

- Read the poem again, encouraging children to join in on the rhyming words.

Shared Reading

LAB, p. 123

Preview and Predict
- Display *Hunky Dory Found It*. Read aloud the title and the names of the author and the illustrator.

- Discuss the cover illustration with children. Ask what kind of pet Hunky Dory is. Elicit that Hunky Dory is a dog who likes to run off with things.

- Read pages 4-11 for children. Ask what children think this story will be about.

Read Together
- Read the selection aloud, pausing occasionally to ask children to predict what they think will happen next.

- Help children note that the pattern of the story changes on page 28. Ask what they think Julie will do with the "treasures" Hunky Dory has found.

Personal Response
Have children complete *Literacy Activity Book* page 123 to show what might happen if Hunky Dory, like Mary's little lamb, followed Julie to school one day.

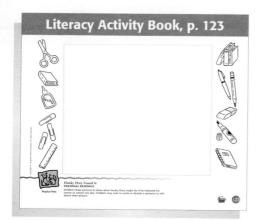

Literacy Activity Book, p. 123

Hunky Dory Found It
PERSONAL RESPONSE
Children draw pictures to show what Hunky Dory might do if he followed his owner to school one day. Children may wish to write or dictate a sentence to tell about their picture.

Playful Pets

Shared Writing: *A Class Story*

Brainstorming

Display page 32 of *Hunky Dory Found It*. Invite children to write a new story about Hunky Dory and the little bear he "finds" on top of Julie Fry's bed. Brainstorm what Hunky Dory might do with the bear.

Drafting

Have children choose one idea they would most like to write about. Then have them dictate sentences for the class story. Print the suggested sentences on chart paper. As you write the name *Hunky Dory*, point out that each word in the dog's name begins with a capital letter. Remind children that names always begin with capital letters.

Publishing

Reread the story with children. Invite volunteers to draw illustrations for it. Save the class story for display during the theme celebration.

Students Acquiring English Shared writing activities give children who are learning English a chance to contribute according to their proficiency levels. They can offer suggestions, chime in, help with illustrations, and/or simply follow along.

Choices for Rereading

Rereadings provide varied, repeated experiences with the literature so that children can make its language and content their own. The following rereading choices appear on page T152.

- Noting Language Patterns
- Echo Reading
- Critical Thinking

Portfolio Opportunity

Save *Literacy Activity Book* page 123 as a record of children's personal response to the story.

2

Interact *with* Literature

BIG BOOK

Sarah Locke dropped a sock.

4

Reading Strategies

▶ **Self-Question/ Monitor**

Discussion Recall with children that good readers *think* as they read. They ask themselves questions about the words, and they reread or look at a picture to help them understand things they don't understand at first.

Ask what Hunky Dory is doing in the picture on pages 4-5. (sniffing in a laundry basket) Point out that the sentence says "Sarah Locke dropped a sock." But the sock isn't shown in this picture. Ask children to look at pages 6-7 and tell what they see hanging on the line. (one sock where there should be two) Ask if they can now figure out what the sentence about Sarah Locke means. (One sock must have fallen as Sarah was hanging up the socks.)

Purpose Setting

Suggest that as children reread the story with you, they look carefully at the pictures for clues about how Hunky Dory "finds" things.

Hunky Dory found it.

6

QuickREFERENCE

Phonics/Decoding Review

Ask children to listen carefully as you read the sentence on page 4. Have them name two words that begin with the sound for *s*. (Sarah, sock) Call on volunteers to frame the words and name the initial consonant.

Phonemic Awareness Review

Have children find two rhyming words on page 4. (Locke, sock)

High-Frequency Word: *it*

TESTED SKILL

Teach/Model

Display Word Card *it*.

Read page 6 for children. Then point to and read Word Card *it*. Ask children to find the word *it* on page 6. Have them match the words letter by letter. Ask:

- What letter does *it* begin with? *(i)*
- What letter does *it* end with? *(t)*

Use Word and Picture Cards to create these sentences in a pocket chart:

I put the [socks] in a [basket].

I put the [socks] in it.

Have children take turns reading the sentences. Help them compare the words *in* and *it*.

Practice/Apply

Have children find the word *it* on pages 10 and 14. Help children read the sentences in which the word appears. Challenge children to name the words that *it* stands for on these pages. *(ball, tie)*

SKILL FINDER High-Frequency Words: *it*, page T158

Background: FYI

The phrase *hunky dory* is a slang expression meaning "quite all right" or "fine." Ask if children think Hunky Dory is a good name for this mischievous mutt.

MEETING INDIVIDUAL NEEDS **Extra Support**

Pronoun Referent Note that the word *it* at the end of the sentence on page 6 stands for the sock that Sarah Locke dropped. Have children paraphrase the sentence, using the words *the sock* instead of *it*.

Interact *with* Literature

Hunky Dory found it.

10

Reading Strategies

▶ **Think About Words**

Display page 9 and discuss how children can figure out the word *ball*.

The story says: *Tommy Hall hit the ___*.

- **What makes sense** The word names something that Tommy Hall hit. I think the word may also rhyme with Tommy's last name: *Hall*.

- **Sounds for letters**

  What letter does the word begin with? *(b)* What word begins with the sound for *b* and rhymes with *Hall*? *(ball)*

- **Picture clues** The picture on pages 8-9 shows a boy trying to catch a ball that another boy has hit. The word is ball.

Reread the sentence on page 9 with children. Ask if *ball* makes sense in this sentence and begins with the sound for *b*.

Quick REFERENCE

High-Frequency Words

Reread the sentence on page 9. Then have children find the word *the* in this sentence.

 Students Acquiring English
MEETING INDIVIDUAL NEEDS

Word Meaning Use the illustration on pages 8 to 9 to help with the meaning of the expression "hit the ball." Then invite volunteers to act it out.

Phonics/Decoding Review

Have children listen for the beginning sound as they say the words *Hall* and *hit*. Ask what letter stands for this sound. *(h)* Then have volunteers read aloud the sentence on page 9.

Tommy Hall
hit the ball.

9

Phonics/Decoding

Phonogram -it

TESTED SKILL

Teach/Model

Remind children that they have learned to read the word *it*. Print *it* on the chalkboard, and have the word read. Then write the letter *h* before *it* to form the word *hit*. Ask:

- What letter does the word now begin with? *(h)*
- What sound does *h* stand for? (/h/)
- What are the sounds for *it*? (/it/)

Have children blend the sounds /h/ and /it/ to read the word *hit*. Then have children find the word *hit* on page 9.

Practice/Apply

Use the letter cards to form these words in a pocket chart, and have children as a group read them.

fit
bit
sit

SKILL FINDER

Phonogram: *-it*, page T156

Background: FYI

Baseball originated in England as a game called *rounders*. Early English settlers in America played rounders, but they called the game by other names, including the "Massachusetts game" and "base ball."

Julie Fry
dropped
Daddy's tie.

12

Hunky Dory found it.

14

Phonics/Decoding Review

Ask children to listen for the sound at the beginning of the words *Daddy's* and *Dory*. What letter stands for this sound? *(d)* Read page 17 and have children name the word that begins with *d*.

Students Acquiring English

MEETING INDIVIDUAL NEEDS

Word Meaning If children are confused, help them find several ties in the picture on pages 12-13. Point out that one meaning for *tie* is a piece of clothing that a boy or man wears around his neck. Ask who the ties in the picture belong to. *(Julie's father)*

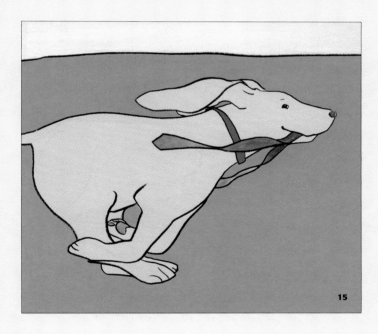

Concepts About Print

End of a Written Word

TESTED SKILL

Teach/Model

Invite children to read the sentence on page 14 with you. Ask them to look carefully at each word. Help them count the words. Then use the word *Hunky* to model how to identify the end of a written word.

Think Aloud

If I look at the letters *H-u-n-k-y*, I see that they are written close together. (Point to these letters.) After the last letter, *y*, I see a space. This space tells me that this is the end of the word (point to the *y* in *Hunky*) and that now another word begins (point to the *D* in *Dory*).

Ask children to show where the next word in the sentence, *Dory*, ends.

Practice/Apply

Continue with the remaining words in the sentence.

SKILL FINDER *Revisiting "In Downtown Philadelphia,"* page T157

Interact
with
Literature

Reading Strategies

 Summarize

Discussion Ask volunteers to summarize what has happened so far in the story. Encourage them to tell:

- who the story is mostly about (Hunky Dory)

- what the problem is (Hunky Dory takes things that he "finds" and runs away with them.)

▶ **Evaluate**

Discussion Ask if children agree that Hunky Dory "finds" things. Help them see the humor in his "finding" things that belong to the people in the story.

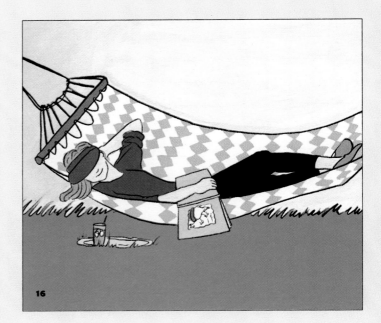

16

Hunky Dory found it.

18

Laurie Cook
put down
her book.

17

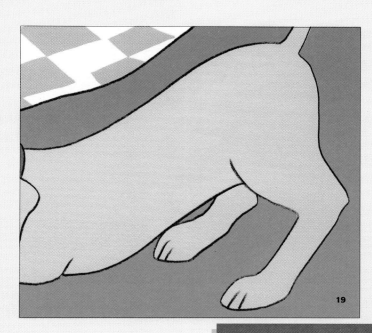

19

Phonics/Decoding

Initial *p*

TESTED SKILL

Teach/Model

Read aloud the sentence on page 17. Frame *put* and remind children that they have learned to read this word. Ask what letter *put* begins with. *(p)* Then ask what sound *p* stands for. (/p/)

Write these words on the board:

    pet   pat

Point to the word *pet*. Ask children to think of a word that makes sense and begins with the sound for *p* to complete this sentence: *Hunky Dory is Julie's ____.*

Repeat the procedure with the word *pat* and the sentence: *Hunky Dory likes a ____ on the head.*

Practice/Apply

Display and help children read the following sentences. Have a volunteer underline the words that begin with /p/*p*.

Patty Scott
dropped a pot.

Hunky Dory found it.

SKILL FINDER *Minilesson Theme 7*

MEETING INDIVIDUAL NEEDS **Challenge**

Antonyms Ask children to suggest a word that means the opposite of *down*. *(up)* Ask a volunteer to pick up a book and to then put it down.

Interact *with* Literature

Reading Strategies

▶ **Monitor**

Discussion Ask if children were puzzled about how Hunky Dory could find a boat. Ask how the pictures on pages 20-21 and 22-23 could help them understand the words on these pages. Children should note that the boat was a toy, and that Hunky Dory swam out into the pond to get it. Discuss how the artist shows that the dog is swimming.

Amy Mote
sailed a boat.

20

22

Hunky Dory
found it.

QuickREFERENCE

Science Link

Ask if children know what makes a boat sail. (the wind) Blow on the sail of a toy sailboat to demonstrate how wind fills the sails and causes the boat to move through the water.

Interact *with* Literature

Reading Strategies

▶ **Monitor**

Discussion Ask what pictures children used to figure out why Baby Sue's mother didn't notice that she had kicked off her shoe. (She was busy picking up the toy that had fallen from the carriage.)

Baby Sue
kicked off
her shoe.

25

Hunky Dory found it.

27

Vocabulary

Idiom Discuss the meaning of *kicked off*. Ask a volunteer to show—gently—how someone might kick off a shoe.

Phonics/Decoding
Initial *k*

Teach/Model

Display Magic Picture *king*.

Discuss how Magic Picture *king* can help children recall the sound for *k*. Have children say *king,* listening for the beginning sound. Then read the sentence on page 25, asking children to listen for a word that begins with the same sound as *king*. Frame the word *kicked*, asking children to name the first letter in the word.

Ask children to say *king* and *kicked*, listening for the beginning sounds.

Practice/Apply

Print these sentences on the board, and help children read them. Ask a volunteer to underline the words that begin with /k/*k*.

<u>Katy</u> Lee
dropped her <u>key.</u>
Hunky Dory found it.

 SKILL FINDER *Decoding k Words, page T155*

Interact
with
Literature

Reading Strategies

▶ **Evaluate**

Discussion Ask if children think Hunky Dory really took the treasures back to their owners. Could a dog do this? Would a dog know to whom each thing belonged? You may want to show children the picture on the back cover of the book to help them draw conclusions about what Hunky Dory may have done with the treasures.

Julie shook her head
and frowned
when she saw
what he had found.

She put the treasures
in a sack.

28

30

QuickREFERENCE

Visual Literacy

Help children identify the various things that Hunky Dory "found" in the picture on pages 28-29.

Extra Support

MEETING INDIVIDUAL NEEDS

Word Meaning Point out the *sack* that Julie put the treasures in. Ask if children call this thing a *sack* or a *bag* or a *tote*. Explain that people who live in different parts of the United States sometimes use different words to name the same thing.

Hunky Dory
took them back.

31

Comprehension
Cause/Effect

TESTED SKILL

Teach/Model

Tell children that often in a story one thing causes another thing to happen. Reread page 28, asking children to listen to find out what caused Julie to shake her head and frown. (She saw the things Hunky Dory had found.)

Write *because* on a sticky note and place it over the word *when* on page 28. Then reread the sentence with children: *Julie shook her head and frowned* because *she saw what he had found.*

Tell children that sometimes the words and pictures in a story tell why things happen. At other times, readers think about what they already know to figure out why things happen.

Help children use what they know about dogs and how they act. Ask: Why did Hunky Dory hide all the things under the bed? (He hid all the things because he is a dog and dogs often like to hide things.)

Practice/Apply

Ask children: Why did Julie put the treasures in a sack? (Julie put them in a sack *because* she wanted Hunky Dory to take them back.)

SKILL FINDER

Why Things Happen, page T154

Minilessons, Themes 3 and 11

Interact *with* Literature

32

Reading Strategies

 Predict/Infer

Discussion Ask children what they think Hunky Dory will do with the bear. Encourage them to give reasons for their answers.

 Evaluate

Discussion Ask if children enjoyed reading this story. Did they think it was funny? Why or why not?

Self-Assessment

Have children ask themselves:
● Did I think about what I know about Hunky Dory and the way he acts to help me predict what he might do next?

QuickREFERENCE

 Home Connection

This would be a good time to invite someone from the community to speak with children about the care and training of pets, especially dogs.

Interact with Literature

Rereading

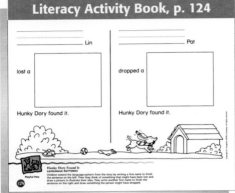

Literacy Activity Book, p. 124

Choices for Rereading

Noting Language Patterns

LAB, p. 124

As you reread the story, help children note the author's use of rhyme and repetition. Point out that each item that someone "loses" rhymes with that person's name: *Sarah Locke/sock; Tommy Hall/ball*, and so on. Ask which sentence is repeated again and again. ("Hunky Dory found it.")

Invite children to help you write a new scene for this story using the language pattern.

Have children complete *Literacy Activity Book* page 124.

Mary Anne
dropped a fan.

Hunky Dory
found it.

Echo Reading

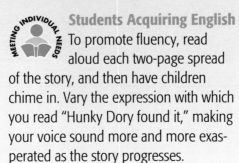

Students Acquiring English
To promote fluency, read aloud each two-page spread of the story, and then have children chime in. Vary the expression with which you read "Hunky Dory found it," making your voice sound more and more exasperated as the story progresses.

Critical Thinking

To focus on story characters' feelings, pause after reading each "Hunky Dory found it." Ask how children think the owner of each object felt when Hunky Dory ran off with it. Ask what children think each owner might have said or done.

Informal Assessment

Use Story Talk or the dramatization activity to assess children's general understanding of *Hunky Dory Found It.*

Responding

Choices for Responding

Story Talk

Have children discuss the following questions in small groups:

- Does *Hunky Dory Found It* remind you of other stories we have read? Which ones? (You might display *Jamaica's Find* to remind children of that story.)

- Do you think Julie should have let Hunky Dory keep all the treasures? Why or why not?

Retelling *Hunky Dory Found It*

Let children work in small groups to retell the story, using the prop board and stick-on retelling pieces. Have the Little Big Books available, so children can check the order in which the objects appear in the story.

> **Materials**
> - Story Retelling Props board and stick-on pieces (See Teacher's Handbook, page H4.)

Personal Response

Invite children to tell about funny things their pets, or their neighbors' pets, have done. Children might draw pictures to show the pets and their antics. Encourage children to write or dictate sentences about their pictures.

Home Connection

Invite children to draw pictures of the various things that Hunky Dory found. Have them label their pictures 1-6 to show the order in which he ran off with each treasure. Children can take their pictures home to retell the story to family members.

3

Instruct and Integrate

Comprehension

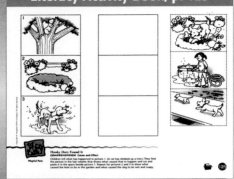

Literacy Activity Book, p. 125

Informal Assessment

As children complete the activities on this page, note their ability to identify the causes of story characters' actions and feelings. Also observe children's recognition of initial /k/k words.

Practice Activities

Why Things Happen

LAB, p. 125

MEETING INDIVIDUAL NEEDS

Extra Support Remind children that often in a story one thing causes another thing to happen. Tell children that one way to figure out what causes something to happen is to ask *Why?* Reread pages 4-7 of *Hunky Dory Found It.* Ask:

- Why did Hunky Dory "find" the sock? (Sarah Locke dropped it; it fell from the line.)

Follow a similar procedure with the text and pictures on these pages:

- pages 8-11: Why did Hunky Dory find Tommy Hall's ball?
- pages 16-19: Why did Hunky Dory find Laurie Cook's book?
- pages 24-27: Why did Hunky Dory find Baby Sue's shoe?

Have children complete *Literacy Activity Book* page 125.

Sound Effects

Help children list sound effects that might be used during a retelling of the story. For each scene, children should name a sound effect and tell what would have caused it. For example:

- pages 4-7: a flapping sound (caused by the wind blowing the clothes on the line)
- pages 8-11: a loud crack (caused by the bat as it hits the ball)

Children may enjoy thinking of ways to create the sound effects they named and including them in a tape recording of a rereading of the story.

More About Hunky Dory

Share *Hunky Dory Ate It* by Katie Evans (Dutton © 1992) with children. Help children identify cause-and-effect relationships in this story by asking questions such as:

- Why did Hunky Dory eat the cake that Clara Lake baked?
- Why did he eat the mudpie that Julie Fry made?
- Why did Hunky Dory begin to feel sick?

Phonics/Decoding

Practice Activities

Literacy Activity Book, p. 127

Decoding *k* Words

LAB, p. 127

Extra Support Display Picture Cards *king, kite, marbles*. Name the pictures with children. Explain that you are going to say a sentence about Hunky Dory and leave out a word. Children should supply the word by saying the picture name that makes sense and begins with the sound for *k*. Read: *Hunky Dory found the ____ I was playing with*.

Discuss why *kite* is the correct choice and why *king* and *marbles* are not. Then repeat the procedure with Picture Cards *sandals, kangaroo, keys* and this sentence: *I dropped my ____, and Hunky Dory found them*. (keys)

Home Connection Have children complete *Literacy Activity Book* page 127 to practice identifying words that begin with /k/*k*. Encourage them to take it home, name the initial *k* words for a family member, and look for another thing from home that might fit in the "boat" with the other items.

Materials

- Picture Cards: *king, kite, marbles; sandals, kangaroo, keys*

My Big Dictionary

Display page 19 of *My Big Dictionary*. Read the words *kangaroo* and *kick* aloud to children, pointing to the initial *k* and emphasizing the /k/ sound as you read. Invite partners to work together to list things on page 19 that begin with the sound for *k*. You may want to encourage children to use temporary spellings and make a list of their words for their Journals.

A Sack Full of Treasures

Place Picture Cards for *k*, together with Picture Cards for *p* and *f*, into a paper bag or sack. Ask children to take turns pretending to be Julie Fry. Each child should pull out a card, name the picture, and tell what letter the picture name begins with. Other children might pretend to be Hunky Dory and say *WOOF!* for each correct response.

My Big Dictionary

Portfolio Opportunity

Save *Literacy Activity Book* page 125 or children's *k* word lists from My Big Dictionary as a record of children's written work.

Instruct *and* Integrate

Phonics/Decoding

Literacy Activity Book, p. 128

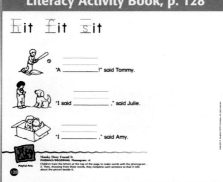

Practice Activities

Phonogram -*it*

Extra Support Ask a volunteer to use the Letter Cards to form the word *bit* in the pocket chart. Ask other children to write *bit* at the top of a sheet of paper. Have children compare what they have written, letter by letter, with the word in the pocket chart. Then ask children to suggest a sentence for the word *bit*.

Continue with other volunteers at the pocket chart as children add these words to their lists: *fit, hit, pit, sit.*

Materials
- Letter Cards: *b, f, h, i, p, s, t*
- pocket chart

I Can Read -*it*

Display the following sentence strips along the chalkboard ledge, and have them read.

> I sit in it.

> I bit it.

> I fit in it.

Provide small groups of children with a set of Picture Cards. Have children take turns choosing and naming a Picture Card, then placing it beside the sentence they might say about that picture.

Practice with -*it*

LAB, p. 128

To provide practice with the phonogram -*it*, have children complete *Literacy Activity Book* page 128.

Challenge Children can work with partners to write sentences for other -*it* words: *bit, kit, pit.*

Materials
- Picture Cards: *banana, bathtub, bus, car, carrot, corn, desk, house, jacket, jeans, jeep, meat, motorcycle, pajamas, pizza, sandwich, seesaw*

Informal Assessment

As children complete the activities, observe their ability to blend consonants with the phonogram -*it*. Also note whether they can identify where words begin and end.

Concepts About Print

Practice Activities

Revisiting "In Downtown Philadelphia"

Extra Support Display the Poster "In Downtown Philadelphia." Invite children to reread the poem with you. Ask a volunteer to frame and read the first word in the first line. Then ask the child how he or she knew where the word *In* ended.

Point to the word *In*. Remind children that the letters in a word are written close together. Note that after the last letter in the word, *n*, there is a space. Recall with children that the space helps tell where one word ends and another begins. Ask volunteers to point to each word in the first verse and name the letter that ends the word.

Ask each child to copy one word from the second verse. Have children circle the letter that ends the word.

Working with Words

Provide small groups of children with a set of the high-frequency words learned to date. Have children in each group take turns choosing a word, reading it, and then pointing to and naming the last letter in the word.

Writing Words

Display the following sentence on the chalkboard:

Hunky Dory found it.

Help children read the sentence. Then ask them to copy it onto a piece of drawing paper, reminding them to put a space between their words. Encourage children to illustrate their sentences.

Instruct *and* Integrate

Vocabulary

Literacy Activity Book, p. 129

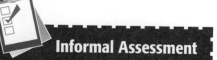

"I have _____," said Hunky Dory.

Ann hit _____.

I put _____ in.

Practice Activities

High-Frequency Words: *it*

Extra Support Display Word Card *it*, and have it read. Remind children that the word *it* takes the place of another word in a sentence. Display the following sentence in the pocket chart:

I put it in the .

Invite children to help you find out what *it* names in each sentence. Display the items. Have a child read the sentence, and then choose the item that *it* names. (pillow) Encourage children to name other things they might put in a bed.

Repeat the procedure by constructing "I put it in the ____" sentences with the other Picture Cards. Continue until all children have a chance to read a sentence and tell what the word *it* names.

Materials

- Picture Cards: *basket, bed, camera, desk, lock, mailbox, sink*
- banana, pillow, roll of film, pencil, keys, newspaper, dish

Hunky Dory Found It

Help children create a rebus list of all the things Hunky Dory found. Then ask children to choose one of the things to draw and write about. Suggest that children show in their drawings what they might put the item they chose in. Have them complete the following sentence frame to label their pictures:

I put it in the _____.

Writing the Word *It*

LAB, p. 129

Have children complete *Literacy Activity Book* page 129 to practice using the word *it* in sentences. Encourage children to share their work with a partner.

Informal Assessment

As children complete the activities on this page, note the ease with which they are able to read the word *it*, as well as other high-frequency words. Also observe whether children can follow oral directions.

Listening

Practice Activities

Hunky Dory Learns a Lesson

Ask children to listen carefully as you describe how to teach a dog to obey a simple command, such as *sit.* Here are the steps:

1. Wave a dog treat once or twice in front of the dog.

2. Hold the treat above and just behind the dog's head. Say the dog's name, followed by the word *sit.*

3. If the dog sits, give it the treat and praise.

4. If the dog does not sit, push gently on its hindquarters to show what you wish it to do.

5. With no treat, say the dog's name and the word *sit.* Again put your hand above and just behind the dog's head.

6. Reward the dog with a treat; repeat ten or so times.

Describe the steps again, asking children to pantomime your instructions.

Listening for Rhyming Words

Remind children that when words end with the same sounds, we say they *rhyme.* To review recognizing the last sounds in spoken words, reread the story, pausing after the second rhyming word in each pair, for example *sock,* to ask: What are the last sounds in *sock:* /s/ or /ock/?

Reread the sentences and ask children to name the word that rhymes with *sock.* (*Locke*) Repeat the procedure with the other rhyming phrases.

Listen and Read!

Audio Tape for Playful Pets:
Hunky Dory Found It

To promote listening skills, place copies of the Little Big Book, along with the Audio Tape, in a quiet area. Invite children to listen to the tape as they follow along in the book.

Portfolio Opportunity

Save children's work from Hunky Dory Found It as a record of their writing the high-frequency word *it.*

Instruct
and
Integrate

Oral Language

Choices for Oral Language

Dramatic Play: At the Vet's

Remind children of the cat Fern from *I Have a Pet!* Talk about how vets help pet owners keep their animals in good health.

Set up a corner of the classroom as a vet's office. Equip it with small notepads that children can use for taking phone messages and for writing prescriptions for sick pets. Place several different kinds of stuffed animals in the corner; these can be used by children as they take their pets to the vet. A toy doctor's kit can also be added, since vets use some of the same tools, such as stethoscopes and thermometers.

Invite children to take turns bringing their pets to the vet. Be sure that the role of the vet changes frequently so that everyone gets a chance to be the pet doctor.

Why Hunky Dory Likes It

Ask children to choose one "treasure" that Hunky Dory ran away with. Ask why the dog might have found the item so enticing. Ask children to use two or three of their Hunky-Dory senses to describe the item. For example:

The Shoe	
Sight	small and white
Smell	old and leathery
Taste	soft and chewy

Big Dogs, Little Dogs

Divide the class into small groups, and give each a picture of a different dog. Identify the breed for children, if need be. Invite groups to talk about their dogs, asking each child in a group to suggest a different describing word that tells about it.

Remeet as a group to talk about the dogs and how children described them. Help children create word webs for their dogs.

Informal Assessment

As children engage in their dramatic play, observe how well their actions and dialogue mimic that of real pet owner's and vets. Also note whether children's writing shows an understanding of letter-sound correspondence.

 # Writing

Choices for Writing

Write a Description

Challenge Suggest that children work with members of their groups from Big Dogs, Little Dogs (page T160) to write a description of the dog in their picture. Ask each child in the group to dictate a sentence as you write it on chart paper.

Before children add the picture of the dog to the chart, you might reread it, or help children reread it, to other groups. Ask if children in other groups can guess what kind of dog is being described.

What If?

Print the following story starter on the chalkboard, and read it with children.

> If I had a dog like Hunky Dory, _____.

Ask children to imagine that Hunky Dory is their pet. Have them work in groups to brainstorm things they might do with such a mischievous pet. Then have children copy the sentence from the board, draw a picture to show what they would do, and then ask for help writing a sentence ending.

Extra Support For an additional writing experience, adapt the activity for an imaginary pet, such as a hippopotamus or a dinosaur.

Lost and Found

Write "Lost and Found" on the board. Have small groups of children create lost-and-found posters of items that Hunky Dory found.

Portfolio Opportunity

Save examples from the writing activities as a record of children's progress with forming letters and their sense of sound-letter correspondence.

3

Instruct *and* Integrate

Cross-Curricular Activities

Working Dogs

The first domestic dogs were working animals rather than pets. Talk with children about some of the things dogs do today to help people. You might mention, if children don't, guide dogs, seeing-eye dogs, rescue dogs, sled dogs, and herding dogs, such as collies, or hunting dogs, such as pointers.

Have children help you collect pictures of dogs that help people. If someone in your community can tell children about the training that these dogs require, invite that person to visit your class. Or, write for information:

Leader Dogs for the Blind
1039 South Rochester Road
Rochester, MI 48307

The Seeing Eye, Inc.
Motion Picture Services
P.O. Box 252
Livingston, NJ 07039

Math

Treasure Measure

Place the items in a sack. Ask children to close their eyes, reach into the sack, and feel the items. Ask them to estimate how many there are. Record children's estimations on chart paper. Then display all the items in the sack, and ask children to count them to validate their estimations.

Divide the class into groups, and give one item and several dog biscuits to each group. Show children how to measure the item, using a dog biscuit as a unit of measure. Have children record and compare their measurements.

Challenge If children are fairly adept at measuring, you might give one group a few larger biscuits, and ask children to remeasure the item. Have them compare how many small-bone units long the item is with its length in big-bone units.

Materials
- small items, such as a sock, a ball, a tie, a book, a toy boat, a baby's shoe
- a sack large enough to hold all the items
- dog biscuits (small-dog size)

Art

Pets in Paintings

Take children on an imaginary visit to an art museum. Show two or three reprints of master paintings that include pets. Ask children to respond to the paintings by telling how they think the artist felt about the animal—and how the painting makes *them* feel. (This activity will help prepare children for the next theme book—*Snow on Snow on Snow*—which is illustrated with oil paintings created by a world-renowned artist.)

NOTE: A wonderful reference for this activity is *Come Look with Me: Animals in Art* by Gladys S. Blizzard (Thomasson-Grant © 1992).

Materials
- reprints of masterpieces that feature pet animals, such as "Goldfish" by Henri Matisse; "The Favorite Cat," lithograph by Nathaniel Currier; or "Still Life with Three Puppies" by Paul Gauguin

Choices for Science

What Is Wind?

Ask children to find pictures in *Hunky Dory Found It* that show how wind can help people do things, such as the laundry on the clothesline on pages 6-7 and the sailboat moving through the water on pages 20-21. Discuss that wind is moving air. We can't see air, but we can see the effects of it when it moves things. Ask children to find in magazines pictures of the *effects* of wind.

Caring for Animals

Make available several simple books about pet care and/or training. Share the books with children. Discuss things about caring for any pet, such as feeding, cleaning, and exercising. You may want to list these on chart paper and post in the Pet Corner.

BIG BOOK

SELECTION:

Snow on Snow on Snow

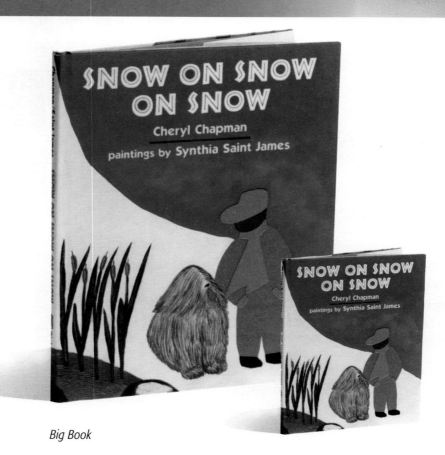

Big Book

Little Big Book

by Cheryl Chapman
illustrated by
Synthia Saint James

**Other Books by
Cheryl Chapman**

Pass the Fritters, Critters

• **Child Study Children's Books of the Year**
• **Booklist Editors' Choice**
• **CCBC Choices**

Selection Summary

A boy and his dog go out into the snow one day. It's a perfect day for sledding with friends. Clancy seems to enjoy the ride down the hill as much as his owner does, but then when they spin out at the end, the dog disappears. Tears on tears on tears freeze the boy's face until he finally hears a woof—coming from below drifts below drifts below drifts of snow.

Lesson Planning Guide

	Skill/Strategy Instruction	Meeting Individual Needs	Lesson Resources
1 **Introduce** *the* **Literature** *Pacing: 1 day*	**Shared Reading and Writing** Warm-up/Build Background, T166 Shared Reading, T166 Shared Writing, T167	Choices for Rereading, T167	**Poster** First Snow, T166 *Literacy Activity Book* Personal Response, p. 130
2 **Interact** *with* **Literature** *Pacing: 1-2 days*	**Reading Strategies** Predict/Infer, T168, T170, T176 Monitor, T168, T174, T180 Think About Words, T172 Evaluate, T176, T182 **Minilessons** Initial *f*, T169 ✔ End of a Written Line, T173 ✔ High-Frequency Words: *did*, T175 ✔ Initial *c*, T177 ✔ Sequence of Events, T181	**Students Acquiring English,** T169, T172, T176, T178, T184, T185 **Extra Support,** T168, T170, T171, T174, T179, T182 **Challenge,** T173, T177, T180, T185 **Rereading and Responding,** T184-T185	**Story Props,** T185, H5 *Literacy Activity Book* Language Patterns, p. 131 See the Houghton Mifflin **Internet** resources for additional activities.
3 **Instruct** *and* **Integrate** *Pacing: 1-2 days*	**Reading/Listening Center** Comprehension, T186 Phonics/Decoding, T187-T188 Concepts About Print, T189 Vocabulary, T190 Listening, T191 **Independent Reading & Writing,** T192-T193 **Language/Writing Center** Oral Language, T194 Writing, T195 **Cross-Curricular Center** Cross-Curricular Activities, T196-T197	**Extra Support,** T186, T187, T188, T189, T190	**Game** Silly Pet Lotto, T188, H8 **Poster** Oh Where, Oh Where Has My Little Dog Gone? T197 **Letter, Word, and Picture Cards,** T187, T188 **My Big Dictionary,** T187 *Literacy Activity Book* Comprehension, p. 132 Phonics/Decoding, p. 133 Vocabulary, p. 134 Tear-and-Take, pp. 135-136 **Audio Tape** for Playful Pets: *Snow on Snow on Snow* See the Houghton Mifflin **Internet** resources for additional activities.

✔ *Indicates Tested Skills. See page T109 for assessment options.*

1

Introduce *the* Literature

Shared Reading and Writing

Poster

FIRST SNOW

Snow makes whiteness where it falls.
The bushes look like popcorn-balls.
And places where I always play,
Look like somewhere else today.

MARIE LOUISE ALLEN

INTERACTIVE LEARNING

Warm-up

Sharing a Poem
- Read aloud "First Snow."

- Invite children to share their experiences with snow. If you live in an area that doesn't receive snow, encourage discussion of the poster.

- Read the poem again as children follow along. Explain that the next book children will read, *Snow on Snow on Snow*, is about a boy and a dog named Clancy who go out in the snow.

 ## Shared Reading
LAB p. 130

Preview and Predict
- Display the covers (front and back) of *Snow on Snow on Snow*. Read the title, as well as the names of the author and the illustrator. You may want to point out that the pictures in this book are oil paintings.

- Invite children to talk about the cover illustration. Ask what they think the words *snow on snow on snow* mean. Elicit that the snow on the cover seems to be piled up very high.

- Read aloud pages 3-11 of the story. Ask children to predict what the boy and his dog will do in the deep snow. If children have not had personal experiences with snow or sledding, use the following Think Aloud.

Think Aloud

On page 11, I see the boy pulling a sled, on which his dog is sitting. I think the boy and his dog plan to have fun in the snow. Maybe they will go sledding down a hill with some friends.

Read Together
- Read the selection aloud, displaying the illustrations and inviting children's reactions.

- Pause after pages 18-19 to ask if children can guess where the dog, Clancy, might have gone.

- Pause again after pages 26-27 to ask how the boy feels, and whether or not he will find his dog. Then read to the end of the story to find out if children's predictions are correct.

Choices for Rereading

Rereadings enable children to make a story's language patterns and content their own. The following rereading choices appear on page T184.

- Noting Language Patterns
- Cooperative Reading
- Characters' Feelings

Personal Response

Have children complete *Literacy Activity Book* page 130 to show their favorite scenes from the story. Suggest that children copy the title from the front cover of the Big Book.

Shared Writing: *A Class "Clancy" Story*

Brainstorming

Invite children to write a new story about Clancy and his owner. Ask them to suggest places where the boy and his dog might go.

to a beach
to a park
to school

Have children choose one idea that they think would make a good story. To help them decide, ask what might happen to Clancy at each place they've suggested.

Drafting

Ask volunteers to dictate sentences for the class story. Record the sentences on chart paper, saying the words as you write them. Ask children to supply the initial consonant when you spell words that begin with sounds they have learned about.

Publishing

Encourage children to make a mural to show various scenes in their story. Decide how many panels will be needed (depending on the number of scenes that children wish to illustrate). Number the panels. Then cut apart the sentences on chart paper to make sentence strips. Display the strips above the appropriate panels.

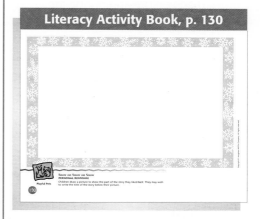

Literacy Activity Book, p. 130

Portfolio Opportunity

Save examples of the writing children do independently on self-selected topics.

Interact *with* Literature

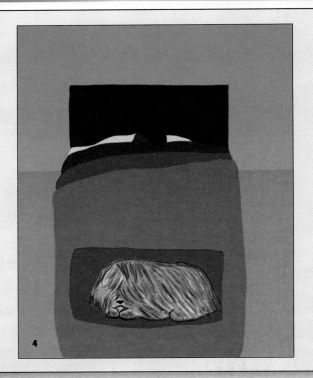

4

6

Reading Strategies

▶ **Predict/Infer**

Monitor

Student Application Remind children that good readers make predictions about what might happen in a story and that they stop from time to time to think over what they have read so far. Recall with children how they used these strategies while reading *I Have a Pet!* and *Hunky Dory Found It.*

Recall with children the predictions they made before and during the reading of *Snow on Snow on Snow*. Ask how making predictions made the story more enjoyable to read. Then ask children if they have any questions about the story that weren't answered in the first reading. Record these questions on chart paper.

Purpose Setting

Invite children to reread the story with you to find answers to their questions.

Quick REFERENCE

Extra Support

Reread the first line on page 5. Ask if the words sound familiar to children. Recall that many folk and fairy tales begin with "once upon a time."

Vocabulary

Word Meanings Point out the word *I* to help children name the boy as the storyteller. Next, relate the phrase *under blankets under blankets under blankets* to the idea of a pile of blankets covering the boy.

Once upon a winter's day
I woke up
under blankets under blankets under blankets.

5

At breakfast
Mama filled up my plate
with food next to food next to food.

Phonics/Decoding
Initial *f*

Teach/Model

Read aloud the sentence on page 7. Then write the words *filled* and *food* on the chalkboard, and read them for children. Ask children to listen for the beginning sound as they say the words. Ask what letter stands for the sound /f/. *(f)*

Practice/Apply

Ask children to listen for a word that begins with the sound for *f* as you read the text on page 12. Frame the word *found* and have the initial letter named. Repeat the procedure with the sentence on page 26. After children identify the word *face*, frame it and have the initial letter named.

SKILL FINDER Minilessons, Theme 7

Visual Literacy

Discuss with children that even though they can't see the faces of the boy, his mother, or the dog, they can name the characters by their shapes. Ask if children can tell what kind of dog the boy's pet is. (sheepdog)

 Students Acquiring English

Position Words Help children understand the phrase *next to*. Ask a volunteer to point out the child sitting *next to* him or her. Then ask children to point out foods on the plate that are next to one another.

★★★ Multicultural Link

Mention that people in different parts of the world eat different foods for breakfast. For example, in China and Japan people usually have tea and rice as part of their breakfasts. Have children talk about their favorite breakfast foods.

Interact *with* **Literature**

BIG BOOK

I pulled on clothes over clothes over clothes.

8

We stepped out the door into snow on snow on snow.

10

Reading Strategies

▶ **Predict/Infer**

Student Application Read through page 9 and ask:

- What kind of weather do you think the boy is dressing for? What clues on pages 8 and 9 let you know? Was there an earlier clue that would help you guess the weather outside? (winter day, blankets under blankets under blankets, pulled on clothes over clothes over clothes)

Talk with children about how the boy is putting on layers of clothing. This would make him nice and warm. Discuss the kinds of weather people can expect in winter.

 Extra Support

Idiom Talk about the phrase *pulled on* and how it lets the reader know that the more clothes the boy put on the harder it was to put on the next layer. Talk about pulling on rain boots over socks and shoes or a jacket over a bulky sweater.

Math Link

Have children count the number of shirt layers the boy has pulled on.

9

11

Science Link

Ask if children know how snow is formed. Explain that snow is formed when water in clouds gets very cold and freezes. It freezes into little crystals which stick together to make snowflakes.

MEETING INDIVIDUAL NEEDS **Extra Support**

Pronoun Referents Help children understand that *we* names just the boy and his dog, even though his mother is also shown. Note that the text says *we stepped into snow* and that only the boy and the dog are stepping in the snow.

2

Interact
with
Literature

Reading Strategies

▶ **Think About Words**

Display page 12 of the story. Talk about how children can figure out the word *hill*.

The story says: *We climbed up the ___ up the ___ up the ___.*

- **What makes sense** The first part of the sentence says that the boy and his dog climbed up. I want to figure out what they climbed. I know that the boy is outdoors, and that he might have climbed a hill, a mountain, or a tree.

- **Sounds for letters** Point to the word *hill,* asking children to identify its beginning letter. Have children say the words *hill, mountain,* and *tree,* listening for the beginning sound. Which word begins with the sound for *h?* (hill)

- **Picture clues** The picture shows the boy and his dog climbing up what looks like a big pile of snow. I think it is a hill covered with snow. The word must be *hill.*

Have children reread the sentence with you to confirm that *hill* makes sense and begins with the sound for *h.*

We climbed
up the hill up the hill up the hill
and found our friends...

12

on sleds beside sleds beside sleds.

14

QuickREFERENCE

Visual Literacy

Ask children what action shown in the pictures shows the opposite of *climbing up.* (sledding down) Have children talk about why the boy can't use his sled to go up the hill.

MEETING INDIVIDUAL NEEDS
Students Acquiring English

Pronoun Referents If children are confused, help them to understand that *our* on page 12 refers to the boy and his dog.

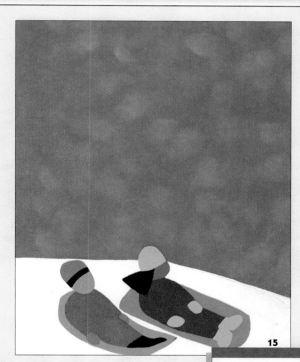

15

Big Book pp. 13, 15

Concepts About Print

End of a Written Line

TESTED
SKILL

Teach/Model

Stand facing the same direction as children and identify first your left hand and then your right. Have children do the same.

Display pages 12-13. Point to the left-hand page and then the right-hand page. Sweep your hand under the first line of type on page 12. Point out where the line begins and where it ends. Help children note that each line of text on page 12 ends near the center of the open book. Ask where it ends on page 14.

Repeat the process, using pages 16-17. Have children note that on page 16, each line of text ends near the center of the book, but on page 17, the text ends toward the edge of the page.

Practice/Apply

Have children practice by pointing out where various lines of text end on subsequent pages of the story.

SKILL FINDER · *Using Sentence Strips,* page T189

MEETING INDIVIDUAL NEEDS

Challenge

Synonyms Ask if children can recall another story word they've read that means the same thing as *beside*. If necessary, turn back to page 7 and reread it. Have children listen for the words that mean nearly the same as *beside*. *(next to)*

Science Link

Tell children the friends have no trouble going down the hill because of something called *gravity*. Explain that gravity keeps everything on Earth from just floating into the air.

Interact
with
Literature

We zoomed
down down down
the slopes,

16

But where <u>did</u> Clancy go?

18

Reading Strategies

▶ **Monitor**

Student Application At this point in the story, the dog is named. Some children may be confused by this and think one of the children is missing, since the focus has been on their activity.

Ask if children were confused about who Clancy was and, if so, how they figured out that he was the dog. (Clancy has appeared in every picture up to this point, but now he is nowhere to be seen.)

Quick**REFERENCE**

Vocabulary

Reread page 16 and ask children which word means "moved very fast." (*zoomed*) Point out that the quick repetition of *down, down, down* helps, too, to convey a sense of fast movement. Relate the word *slopes* to the sides of the hill.

Extra Support

Idiom Ask volunteers to use the picture on page 17 to tell what *spinning out at the end* means. If children need help, mention that *spinning out at the end* means "turning every which way before stopping."

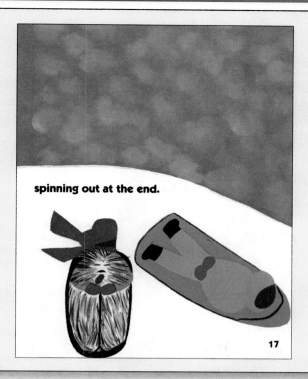

spinning out at the end.

17

19

High-Frequency Words: *did*

TESTED SKILL

Teach/Model

Display Magic Picture *dinosaur*, asking children what sound this picture helps us remember. (the sound for *d*) Ask children to listen as you read page 18 to name a word that begins with the sound for d. (did)

Display Word Card *did*.

Read *did* aloud, emphasizing the initial consonant. Call on a volunteer to frame the word *did* on the page and name the initial letter.

Invite children to help you read the page, pausing for them to supply the word *did*.

Practice/Apply

Display this sentence in a pocket chart:

My did it.

Have children read the sentence; then remove the picture and have children suggest other words to put in the blank. Have children read their new sentences.

SKILL FINDER · Reading *Did*, page T190

Math Link

Have children count the children shown on page 19. Have them compare that number to the number of children shown coming down the hill. Is it the same or different?

🖊 Journal

Suggest that children draw pictures in their journals of things they like to do with friends. (Children who have pets might include their pets in their pictures.)

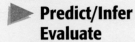

Interact
with
Literature

We looked

behind trees

behind trees

Reading Strategies

▶ **Predict/Infer**
Evaluate

Student Application Read
pages 20 and 21 and ask:

- Why did the children look
behind trees for Clancy?
Does this make sense?
Would you have done the
same thing? Why or why not?

Then read pages 22 and 23 and
ask:

- If you were with the children
searching, what would you
suggest you all do next
instead of continuing to
search?

Encourage children to share personal knowledge and experiences
that help them evaluate the
friends' actions.

22

QuickREFERENCE

Students
Acquiring English

Pronoun Referents If children are
confused, help them understand that
we refers to the boy and his friends.

behind trees

We searched
around bushes
around thickets
around cattails.

Vocabulary

Tell children that *thickets* is another word for *bushes*. Say, also, that cattails are plants that are named so because they look like cats' tails standing straight up in the air. Invite children to point out the cattails in the picture.

Challenge

Synonyms Reread page 20 and see if children can name a word they hear that means nearly the same as *searched*. *(looked)*

Phonics/Decoding

Initial *c*

TESTED SKILL

Teach/Model

Display Magic Picture *cat*.

Invite children to talk about how Magic Picture *cat* can help them remember the sound for *c*. Then ask children to listen for a word that begins with the same sound as *cat* as you read page 23. Frame *cattails*, and have the first letter named. *(c)*

Have children listen for another word that begins with /k/ as you reread page 29. Frame the word *came* and have the initial letter named.

You may want to mention that the sound /k/ is also spelled with the letter *k*, as in *king*.

Practice/Apply

Read aloud these sentences, asking children to raise their hands when they hear a word that begins with the same sound as *cat*. Have a volunteer say the word. Write it on the chalkboard, then have the child point to the initial *c*.

It's cold outside.
The cup of soup is warm.

SKILL FINDER — Decoding *c* Words, page T187

Interact
with
Literature

BIG BOOK

Clancy had disappeared
into the snow
into the wind
into the air.

24

Tears on tears on tears
froze my face.

QuickREFERENCE

MEETING INDIVIDUAL NEEDS

Students Acquiring English

Word Meanings Help children to use the picture and word clues to understand that *disappeared* means out of sight or gone.

25

27

MEETING INDIVIDUAL NEEDS

Extra Support

Word Meaning Have children tell how they know the boy was crying. (tears) Ask if he was crying a lot or a little and how they know. (a lot, repetition of tears)

Science Link

Tell children that water begins to freeze at a temperature of 32 degrees Fahrenheit. Use a large indoor or outdoor thermometer to show the 32 degree mark. Ask what might happen if it were raining and the temperature dropped to below 32 degrees.

Interact *with* Literature

28

Reading Strategies

▶ **Monitor**

Student Application After reading pages 28-30, encourage children to tell how they figured out Clancy had been found. You might guide their thinking by asking:

- What kind of animal says *woof*? What kind of animal is Clancy?

- Does it make sense that the children searched and searched and couldn't see a big dog like Clancy? What clues are given in the story?

- What might Clancy have been doing while the children looked for him? Why do you think that?

Vocabulary

To help children understand *drifts of snow,* explain that wind can blow snow into big piles called *snow drifts.*

 Challenge

Synonyms Have children use the picture to help them think of a word they could use in place of *below.* (under)

★★★ Multicultural Link

Ask what other sounds dogs make. (*ruff, bow wow, arf*) Invite children from other language backgrounds to share words they know for dog sounds, such as: Chinese—*wung, wung;* Spanish—*gua, gua;* French—*woa, woa;* Russian—*gav, gav.*

**Below drifts below drifts below drifts of snow
there came a woof.**

29

31

Comprehension

Sequence of Events

TESTED SKILL

Teach/Model

Talk briefly with children about some of the things you and they have done so far in class. Describe them in the order in which they occurred. Remind children that just like in real life, things in a story happen in a certain order.

Retell the story in your own words. Then ask children what was the very first thing that happened in the story. (The boy woke up and ate breakfast.) Ask what happened next. (He got dressed to go outside.) Have children recall what happened then. (He went out into the snow to go sledding.) Repeat the sequence of events children identified, using words such as *first*, *next*, *then*.

Practice/Apply

Talk through the remainder of the story, asking children to volunteer the story events in correct order. When all the events have been stated, repeat the sequence for children.

SKILL FINDER

Sequence of Events, page T186

Minilessons, Themes 1, 3, 7, and 11

Interact *with* Literature

Reading Strategies

▶ **Evaluate**

Student Application Invite children to tell if they think the events in this story could happen in real life. Discuss their responses.

Then ask how many children would tell their friends to read this story. Have them tell why. If some children did not like the story, encourage them to tell why. Invite these children to tell how the story might be made better.

And
we all lived
happily
ever after ever after ever after.

32

Self-Assessment

Children can self-assess by asking:

- While I'm reading, do I think about what I know from the words in the story and what I know from the pictures to help me understand what is happening?

- If I didn't understand something when I was reading, did I stop and reread or ask someone for help?

Quick**REFERENCE**

 Extra Support

Storytelling Language Ask children if the ending of the story sounds familiar. Where have they heard it before? Point out that just as the story began with the fairy-tale words "Once upon a," it ends like a fairy tale, too.

2

Interact with Literature

Rereading

Literacy Activity Book, p. 131

Once upon a winter's day

Once upon a summer's day

Choices for Rereading

Noting Language Patterns

LAB p. 131

As you read the story, ask children to raise their hands when they hear words repeated. Help children see that almost every sentence includes a phrase that is said three times. Help children find a few examples.

- page 5: under blankets under blankets under blankets
- page 7: food next to food next to food
- page 12: up the hill up the hill up the hill

Have children complete *Literacy Activity Book* page 131 to tell what they once did on a winter's day and on a summer's day.

Cooperative Reading

Students Acquiring English
Invite children to read the story with you. They can supply the repeated prepositional phrases. If necessary, prompt by reading the first phrase, and invite children to join in on the repetitions.

Characters' Feelings

As you reread the story, ask children to tell how they think the boy feels at various points. Logical places to pause for their responses are after pages 11, 15, 18, 26, 29, and 32.

Informal Assessment

Use Story Talk or the Retelling activity to assess children's general understanding of *Snow on Snow on Snow*.

Responding

Choices for Responding

Personal Response

Encourage children to draw pictures to show what they would do if it snowed *snow upon snow upon snow.* If you live in an area of the country where it doesn't snow or snow is infrequent, you might ask children to use their imaginations to think what they would like to do if they could travel to a place where there was lots of snow.

Story Talk

Talk with children in small groups about the following questions:

- Imagine that you are the boy in the story. How would you have felt when you couldn't find Clancy? What would you have done?

- What do you think the boy will do next time it snows? Will he take Clancy with him? Why or why not?

- What do you think Hunky Dory would have done if he had been the boy's pet?

Retelling *Snow on Snow on Snow*

Invite children to work in small groups to use the story props to retell the story. Encourage them to use some of the repeated phrases from the text in their retellings.

Students Acquiring English Place children acquiring English in English–speaking groups. These children can follow the lead of other group members and chime in on the repeated phrases.

Materials
- Story Retelling Props repeating images (See Teacher's Handbook, page H5.)

Another Point of View

Challenge Encourage children to retell *Snow on Snow on Snow* from Clancy's point of view. Page through the story with them, asking what Clancy might be "thinking" at various points. What might Clancy say, if he could talk?

Portfolio Opportunity

Save the language pattern activity on *Literacy Activity Book* page 131 as a record of children's work. Also keep their work from Personal Response.

Instruct
and
Integrate

Comprehension

Literacy Activity Book, p. 132

Practice Activities

Sequence of Events

LAB, p. 132

Extra Support Review with children what happened in *Snow on Snow on Snow*:

- at the beginning (The boy got up and ate breakfast.)

- in the middle (The boy and Clancy went sledding; Clancy got lost in the snow.)

- at the end (Clancy was found and they all lived happily ever after.)

Show children how to fold a piece of paper into three sections. Have them write the numbers 1, 2, and 3 at the top. Then ask children to draw what happened at the beginning of the story under number 1. Have them draw what happened in the middle under number 2. Have them draw what happened at the end under number 3. Ask children to use their pictures to retell the story to a partner.

Have children complete *Literacy Activity Book* page 132.

Which Came First?

Ask children to listen as you reread two sentences from the story. Read:

- *At breakfast Mama filled up my plate with food next to food next to food.*

- *I woke up under blankets under blankets under blankets.*

Ask if children can recall which sentence tells something that happened first in the story. If needed, read the two sentences again. Discuss that the boy woke up first; then he ate breakfast.

Repeat with other sentence pairs from the story.

Order Words

Ask children to listen as you briefly retell *Snow on Snow on Snow*.

> *First,* I got out of bed.
> *Then* I ate breakfast.
> Clancy and I found our friends.
> *Next,* we went sledding.
> Clancy fell into a deep snow bank.
> *Finally,* I heard a woof.

Explain that some words, like *first, then, next,* and *finally,* are clues to when things happen. Reread the summary, sentence by sentence. Pause after each sentence with an italicized word, asking children to name the word that tells when.

Informal Assessment

As children complete the activities, note their ability to identify sequence of events. Also observe their recognition of initial /k/c words.

Phonics/Decoding

Practice Activities

Decoding *c* Words

LAB, p. 133

Extra Support Write this sentence on the chalkboard, underlining as shown:

"I have a pet <u>cat</u>," said Pat.

Below the sentence, display Picture Cards *cat, dog, cane*. Read the sentence for children and leave out the word *cat*. Children should supply the word by saying the picture name that makes sense and begins with the sound for *c*.

Repeat the procedure with Picture Cards *car, comb, mailbox* and this sentence: *"Put it in the car," said Dad*.

Have children complete *Literacy Activity Book* page 133.

Materials
- Picture Cards: *cat, dog, cane; car, comb, mailbox*

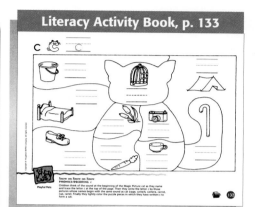

Literacy Activity Book, p. 133

My Big Dictionary

Display pages 8-10 of *My Big Dictionary*. Read the words on page 8 aloud to children, pointing to the initial *c* and emphasizing the /k/ sound as you read. Invite partners to work together to find five things on page 11 that begin with the sound for *c*. You may want to encourage children to use temporary spellings and make a list of their words for their Journals.

"C" Word Collage

Invite children to help you make a collage of /k/*c* words. Children can look through old magazines and cut out pictures whose names begin with /k/. If children select pictures whose names begin with the letter *k* instead of *c*, place these aside, explaining that sometimes the /k/ sound is spelled with a *k*. Later, children can make a collage of the /k/*k* pictures. Help children label the pictures. Display the collages on the word wall.

My Big Dictionary

Portfolio Opportunity

Save *Literacy Activity Book* page 133 as a written record of children's work on initial /k/*c* words. Also keep their sequence drawings to record their understanding of the comprehension skill.

Instruct *and* Integrate

Phonics/Decoding

Practice Activities

Initial Sound Review

Prepare for children simple 2 X 2 grid "Bingo" cards of the initial consonants they have learned so far. Tell children that you will hold up a Picture Card and name it. They are to listen for the beginning sound and think of the letter(s) that stand for that sound. If children see the letters on their cards, they should cover them with markers. The first child to cover all the letters on his or her card wins.

c/k	m
p	g

s	d
c/k	f

b	f
c/k	h

Materials
- Picture Cards: *bear, bird, camel, cat, dog, duck, fish, fox, goat, hippopotamus, horse, kangaroo, monkey, mouse, pig, seal*

Silly Pet Lotto

Materials
- Game: Silly Pet Lotto (See Teacher's Handbook, page H8.)

Let children play the game with partners to practice initial /k/c and other initial consonants they have learned.

 ### Home Connection

Recall with children how the boy's mother filled his plate *with food next to food next to food.* Suggest that children work with their families to make a list of foods that begin with the sound for *c*, as in *cookie*. Children can then bring their lists into school to share their findings. You'll be amazed at the feast! Here is a sampling:

caramel	corn
cauliflower	cucumber
cocoa	cupcake
coconut	custard
cookie	

Informal Assessment

As children complete the activities on page T189, note their ability to track words in a sentence from left to right and to identify the end of a written line.

Concepts About Print

Practice Activities

Using Sentence Strips

Extra Support Prepare sentence strips for several pages of the story. Give the strips to children. Then, as you reread the story aloud, have them rebuild the text in a pocket chart.

> Once upon a winter's day
>
> I woke up
>
> under blankets under blankets under blankets.

> At breakfast
>
> Mama filled up my plate
>
> with food next to food next to food.

Read the sentences with children, sweeping your hand under the words with a left-to-right motion. Call on volunteers to point to the last word in each line.

End of a Written Line

Reread *Hunky Dory Found It* with children. Pause after the following pages to ask where the last line of type ends: near the center of the book or near the edge of the right-hand page: page 7, 8, 17, 18, 24, and 26.

Sharing Favorite Little Big Books

Invite partners to revisit their favorite Big Books. Provide partners with copies of the Little Big Books and a package of sticky notes. As children read the stories, have them place a sticky note at the end of each line of text.

3

Instruct *and* Integrate

Vocabulary

Practice Activities

Reading *did*

LAB p. 134

 Extra Support Display the following sentences, and have children read them:

It did go.   I did go in.   I did it!

Ask children to tell what might cause someone to say each of these sentences.

Suggest that children copy one of the sentences onto drawing paper. Invite them to illustrate their sentences.

Have children complete *Literacy Activity Book* page 134.

It's Snowing Words!

Write all the high-frequency words children have learned thus far on snowflakes cut from white paper.

Have children take turns choosing a word, reading it, and then pasting it onto a bulletin board covered beforehand with bright blue paper.

Children might add other "wordflakes" to the bulletin board to show other words they know or would like to learn.

Reading *did* and *it*

Display Word Cards *did* and *it,* and have children practice reading them. Then display Word Cards for all the high-frequency words children have learned thus far.

Invite children to take turns forming sentences from the words. Allow children to add Picture Cards, if they'd like to. Then have children copy and illustrate their sentences.

Tear-and-Take Story

LAB pp. 135-136

Have children remove the *Literacy Activity Book* page, fold it to make a book, and read the story. Suggest that children take the book home to read to their families.

Sit, Kit!

Informal Assessment

As children read the Tear-and-Take story and complete other activities, note how readily they are able to identify the high-frequency words. Also observe how well children listen and respond to questions.

Listening

Practice Activities

Pet Ideas

Share with children information about where the authors of the theme books got their ideas for the stories.

- Shari Halpern got the idea for *I Have a Pet!* by watching her own cat, Fern, which looks just like the one in the story. Fern sits on her owner's desk and watches as Shari Halpern cuts out the tiny pieces of paper that make up her illustrations.

- Katy Evans was inspired by her family's dog to write both *Hunky Dory Ate It* and *Hunky Dory Found It.*

- Cheryl Chapman got the idea for *Snow on Snow on Snow* from the words of a song. (The song, "In the Bleak Midwinter," was sung by Pierce Pettis.) The words of the song came from a poem written long ago by Christina Rossetti.

Ask children to talk about things their pets or neighbors' pets do that might give them ideas for their own writing.

Listen and Read!

 Audio Tape for Playful Pets: *Snow on Snow on Snow*

Suggest that children listen again to the tape for *Snow on Snow on Snow.* You might ask children to listen for the way in which the narrator reads the repeated phrases.

Ask Clancy!

Have children brainstorm a list of questions they might like to ask Clancy about his day out in the snow. Record their suggestions on chart paper. Then have children take turns asking the questions while a volunteer plays the part of Clancy—and responds in words as well as in woofs.

Portfolio Opportunity

Save sentences from Reading *did* and *it* as a record of children's work with the high-frequency words.

3
Instruct and Integrate

Independent Reading & Writing

The Cake

The Cake
by John Edward Valdez

This story provides practice and application for the following skills:

- **High-Frequency Words:** *did, it*
- **Phonics/Decoding Skills:** Initial *c* and *k*; phonogram *-it*
- **Cumulative Review:** Previously taught decoding skills and High-Frequency Words

INTERACTIVE LEARNING

Independent Reading

Watch Me Read

Preview and Predict

- Display *The Cake*. Point to and read the title and the author's and illustrator's names.

- Invite children's comments on the cover illustration. Have them name the pets—Dog, Cat, Bird, Hamster—and tell where the pets are.

- Preview pages 1-3, noting that a bite is missing from the cake.

- Invite children to predict who "bit" the cake.

Read the Story

- Suggest that children read independently to see if their predictions match the story.

- After reading the story ask:
  Who bit the cake?
  Is this how you thought the story would end?

Rereading

- Invite children to reread the story aloud, using their voices to show how the animals feel. You might demonstrate how to read in an upset or an accusatory manner for children.

- Have small groups of children reread the story for a Reader's Theater performance. Suggest that children practice reading their lines in their groups before reading the story for the class.

Responding

- Encourage children to draw and write about a pet from the story they would like to have.

- Ask children to draw a new ending for the story. Have them use the story pattern to label their drawings: *"I did," said (animal's name)*.

Student Selected Reading

Favorite Big Books

Encourage children to reread Big Books from previous themes. Children might read the books independently or with partners. You may also want to make the Little Big Books available to children for rereading in small groups.

Books for the Library Corner

Display several of the Books for the Library Corner suggested in the Bibliography on page T104. You may want to give Book Talks for a few of these titles. Then invite children to read the books, or browse through them, during their leisure time.

Student Selected Writing

My Own Words

Suggest that children add to their picture dictionaries words they enjoy or use often in their writing. Children may want to add a special page for words that name and/or describe different kinds of pets.

Reading Logs

Encourage children to keep reading logs. During scheduled writing time, they can respond to the pet stories they read and listen to. Children can respond by drawing pictures of the featured pets and/or by writing their reactions to the stories. Allow children to use temporary spellings as they write in their logs.

Books for Independent Reading

The Cake
by John Edward Valdez

Children may also enjoy rereading the WATCH ME READ titles from earlier themes.

Hunky Dory Found It
by Kati Evans
illustrated by Janet Morgan Stoeke

Snow on Snow on Snow
by Cheryl Chapman
illustrated by Synthia Saint James

Have children read these books independently or with a partner. Children may also enjoy rereading the Little Big Book titles from previous themes.

See the Bibliography on pages T104-T105 for more theme-related books for independent reading.

Ideas for Independent Writing

- an **invitation** to the theme celebration
- a **description** of a pet, real or imaginary
- a **thank-you note** to someone who has visited the class to tell about pets and their care and/or training

Portfolio Opportunity

Save examples of the writing children do independently on self-selected topics.

**Instruct
and
Integrate**

Oral Language

Choices for Oral Language

Here's What I Can Do!

Encourage each child to choose an activity associated with having or caring for a pet. Ask children to take turns telling classmates how that activity is properly done. Children might choose from the following:

- shampooing a dog
- brushing a dog or a cat
- cleaning out a pet's cage
- feeding a pet
- walking a dog properly—on a lead
- teaching a parakeet to talk
- teaching a dog to sit or to come
- taking a pet to the vet

Sun on Sun, Snow on Snow

Divide a bulletin board into two sections. Label one side of the bulletin Sun on Sun on Sun and the other side Snow on Snow on Snow.

Invite children to find or draw pictures to show what people do in the summer, when days are warmer (sun on sun), and what they do in winter, when it's often cold (with snow on snow). Encourage children to share their pictures with the class, describing what they show. Then have them attach the pictures to the appropriate sentence of the bulletin board.

Sharing Songs and Poems

Point out to children that many songs and poems have been written about pets. Share a few books of pet poems with children. Encourage them to choose their favorites and then to memorize lines they especially like.

Children can recite their favorite poems and sing their favorite songs for the theme celebration pet show.

Using Order Words

Write the order words *first, then, next,* and *last* on the chalkboard. Read the words for children. Ask them to use one or more of the words as they tell what they do:

when they get up in the morning;

when they are in school;

when they go out to play;

when they get ready for bed.

Informal Assessment

Observe children as they role play Clancy and/or ask questions of Clancy to informally assess their understanding of the story. Also note whether children are now confident about writing their own names.

 # Writing

Choices for Writing

Keeping Records

Tell children that many people keep health records for their pets. Sometimes, a vet will give a pet owner a folder in which to keep pictures and other information about their pets. Provide children with a large piece of construction paper. Have them fold the paper in half to make a folder.

Duplicate a Health Record form for children to fill out for a pet they have or would like to have. Suggest that children use their own names and addresses on the form, providing help with spelling as needed. Have children paste their forms on their folders. Children can place pictures and drawings of their pets or their favorite pet writings in the folder.

Health Record

for
_____

Pet's Name
_____

Kind of Pet
_____

Color
_____

Markings
_____

Owner's Name
_____

Address
_____

City   State
_____

Phone

The Perfect Pet

Brainstorm a list of animals children would like to have as pets, no matter how big or small. Help children describe the animals they suggest. Ask questions that elicit words to tell about each animal's size, color, and other features.

Ask children to draw pictures of themselves and their perfect pets. Encourage them to write or dictate sentences about the pets.

Writing Notices

Discuss how the boy in the story felt when he thought Clancy was lost. Ask if children have ever lost a pet. Did they get their pet back? How did they do it?

Then display the Pet Message Board poster. Invite children to write notices for a lost–or found–pet, using the one on the poster as a model. They might include additional information, such as their pet's name and their phone number.

Poster

 **Portfolio Opportunity**

Save children's work from one or more of these activities.

Instruct
and
Integrate

Cross-Curricular Activities

Math

Yummy Pet Licenses

Talk about the importance of having licenses and name-address tags for our pets. Then, in preparation for celebrating the theme, invite children to help you make a batch of yummy pet licenses to serve to their guests.

Allow children to measure the ingredients and help with the mixing. Invite them to take turns rolling the sugar-cookie dough and using the cookie cutter. Poke a small hole at the top of each cookie so that it looks like a dog tag. After cookies are baked, children can "paint" a pet's name on each one, using a mixture of egg yolk, food coloring, and water.

Note that you will need access to an oven for this activity.

Materials
- ingredients for your favorite sugar-cookie dough recipe
- round cookie cutter
- egg yolk, food coloring, water

Social Studies

Make Your Own Compass

Make signs for *north*, *south*, *east*, and *west*, and tape them on the appropriate walls of your class. Discuss the direction words with children.

Display a compass, explaining that it can help a person find his or her way when lost. Show how the compass always points north, no matter which wall you face. Then invite children to help you make a compass.

1 Rub the sewing end of the needle against the end of the magnet several times to magnetize it.

2 Tape the needle to the cardboard.

3 Float the cardboard in water.

Ask children to take turns pushing the needle around. Have them note that the needle, like the compass, turns to always point north.

Materials
- compass
- magnet, sewing needle
- small piece of thick cardboard
- masking tape
- clear bowl filled with water

Music

Sharing a Song

Display the poster for "Oh Where, Oh Where Has My Little Dog Gone?" Remind children that they sang the song when they read *Jamaica's Find*.

Invite children to sing the song with you. Discuss with children how the song goes with both *Jamaica's Find* and *Snow on Snow on Snow*. Then invite children to change the words of the song just a little so that it applies to Clancy in *Snow on Snow on Snow*.

You might write children's suggestions on self-stick notes and place them over the words on the poster that children wish to replace. For example, they might change *little* to *big* in the first line and transpose *short* and *long* in the third line.

Art

Painting with "Snow"

Prepare snow "finger paint" for children by mixing in a large bowl four cups of soap flakes with one cup of water. Beat until the mixture is the consistency of whipped cream.

Give each child a piece of dark construction paper. Children can use the soap-flake mixture as finger paint to create a picture of Clancy. Small pieces of black construction paper can be added for Clancy's nose. After their paintings have dried, invite children to share their pictures with classmates. Encourage them to recall a repeated phrase from the story to help them tell about their pictures.

Materials
- soap flakes (four cups); water
- mixing bowl, beater

Theme Assessment Wrap-Up

ASSESSMENT

Reflecting/Self-Assessment

Copy the chart below to distribute to children. Ask them which stories in the theme they liked best. Then discuss what was easy for them and what was more difficult as they read the selections and completed the activities. Have children put a check mark under either *Easy* or *Hard*.

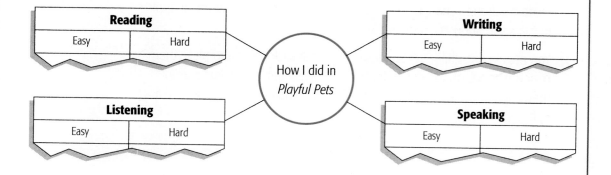

Reading	
Easy	Hard

Writing	
Easy	Hard

How I did in
Playful Pets

Listening	
Easy	Hard

Speaking	
Easy	Hard

Monitoring Literacy Development

There will be many opportunities to observe and evaluate children's literacy development. As children participate in literacy activities, note whether each child has a beginning, a developing, or a proficient understanding of reading, writing, and language concepts. The Observation Checklists, which can be used for recording and evaluating this information, appear in the *Teacher's Assessment Handbook*. They are comprised of the following:

Concepts About Print and Book Handling Behaviors

- Concepts about print
- Book handling

Emergent Reading Behaviors

- Responding to literature
- Storybook rereading
- Decoding Strategies

Emergent Writing Behaviors

- Writing
- Stages of Temporary Spelling

Oral Language Behaviors

- Listening attentively
- Listening for information
- Listening for direction
- Listening to books
- Speaking/language development
- Speaking/language development

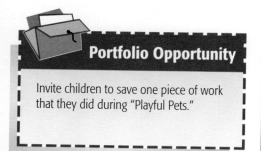

Portfolio Opportunity

Invite children to save one piece of work that they did during "Playful Pets."

Choices for Assessment

Informal Assessment

Review the Observation Checklists and observation notes to determine:

- Did children's responses during and after reading indicate comprehension of the selections?

- How well did children understand the skills presented in this theme? Which skills should be reviewed and practiced in the next theme?

- Did children enjoy the cooperative activities related to the major theme concept?

Formal Assessment

Select formal tests that meet your classroom needs:

- *Kindergarten Literacy Survey*

- Integrated Theme Test

- Theme Skills Test for Playful Pets

See the *Teacher's Assessment Handbook* for guidelines for administering tests and using answer keys and children's sample papers.

Portfolio Assessment

Evaluating Work in the Portfolio

- Periodically review the work in portfolios to determine whether they contain the evidence you need. Ask yourself these questions: 1) Do I have evidence, whether from children's work or observations and anecdotal notes, of the most important things I want children to learn? 2) Do I have enough dated samples to show progress over time?

- Look at several portfolios each week to remind yourself about each child. These private conferences with yourself will help you plan instruction.

- Use the Observation Checklists as a guide when you evaluate work in the portfolio. They will help you focus on important learning goals.

Managing Assessment

Using the Kindergarten Literacy Survey

Question: How can II use the *Kindergarten Literacy Survey* to assess children's progress?

Answer: The *Kindergarten Literacy Survey* can be administered a few times during the year.

- During the first several weeks of school you may want to administer the survey to all your students. This will provide good information for planning instruction and it will provide a good beginning-of-year record.

- As students progress, you may want to administer the survey again as appropriate. Don't try to fit all children into the same timeline. Administer it as children demonstrate facility with the skills included.

- Place the survey in the child's portfolio. Share the information with parents along with other portfolio work.

For more information on the *Kindergarten Literacy Survey* and other topics, see the *Teacher's Assessment Handbook.*

Celebrating the Theme

Choices for Celebrating

Put on a "Pet" Show

Invite children to put on a show in which they share not only their class pet but also their "pet" books and projects for the theme. Children might invite friends and family members to share such things as:

- the class pet and the Pet Corner
- poems and songs about pets
- stories children have written about pets
- pictures of their Perfect Pets

Children who have pets at home might surprise their families by promising to do one new pet-related duty. It might be a simple task, such as filling the dog's water dish twice a day. Prepare simple "contracts" for children to sign, with the task and a place to check off that the job has been done each day.

Alternately, children who don't have pets might offer to do something for a neighbor's pet or take on a new household task.

See the Houghton Mifflin **Internet** for additional theme-related activities.

Self-Assessment

Have children meet in small groups to talk about what they learned in the theme. Use the following prompts to foster their discussion:

- What have you learned about different kinds of pets and how to care for them?
- Do you think caring for your own pet is a job that you are ready for? Why or why not?

Sharing Stories

Invite children to talk about the books they have read and listened to during the theme. Encourage them to describe the pets in each book and to tell how the stories are alike and different. Ask volunteers to work in small groups to retell or dramatize the stories for the rest of the class.

Sharing the Class Pet

Invite another class to visit your room to learn about the class pet. Encourage children to tell their visitors about their pet and how they care for it. If you have made yummy dog licenses, children can share them with their guests.

Teacher's Handbook

TABLE OF CONTENTS

Story Retelling Props

Materials
- stuffed dog
- hat

Jamaica's Find

For *Jamaica's Find,* you may want to bring in a stuffed dog and a hat similar to the red sock hat in the story. Invite children to use the props as they dramatize the story. Encourage them to re-create different scenes from the story with Jamaica, her mother, and Kristin.

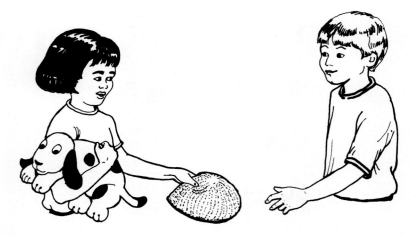

Resources
- stick-on retelling pieces
- prop board

What Shall We Do When We All Go Out?

To help children retell *What Shall We Do When We All Go Out?* lean the prop board against an easel or the chalkboard and make the stick-on retelling pieces available. Invite a boy and a girl to pretend they are the boy and girl in the story. The children can then place the stick-on pieces in the appropriate places on the prop board as they retell the story. Encourage the children to remember the sequence of events in the story, and to recall the repetition and word patterns in the book.

INTERACTIVE LEARNING *(continued)*

What Shall We Do When We All Go Out?

You can create a set of props that will help children recreate the sequence of events in *What Shall We Do When We All Go Out?* Draw or cut and paste a cereal box, a tricycle, a seesaw, a pair of roller skates, a lunch box, a duck, a kite, and a bowl of soup onto separate pieces of oaktag or construction paper. Children will enjoy using these to show what the boy and girl in the book do during the course of their day.

Materials
- oaktag
- construction paper
- crayons or markers
- paste
- scissors

Together

To help children retell the poem *Together,* use 11" x 17" oaktag sheets to create stanza boards. Draw or cut and paste the following pictures for stanza 1: boards/house, cheese/mouse, ice cubes/ice cream freezer, heads together; stanza 2: fire truck/fire, piano keys/musical notes, baseball/baseball caps, heads together; and stanza 3: shovel/pail, paintbrush and boat/sailboat sail, rocks/heads together. For the fourth line of each board, draw an outline of two profiles touching, with one thought balloon. Display the stanza boards one at a time, and help the children recall the poem.

Materials
- oaktag
- crayons or markers
- scissors
- glue

Story Retelling Props

Materials
- paper lunch bags
- crayons or markers
- construction paper
- scissors
- glue

I Have a Pet!

For *I Have a Pet!* decorate lunch bags to create hand puppets for each of the pets in the story: hamster, lizard, dog, cat, parakeet. Then make award ribbons of colored construction paper for: Best Tricks, Softest Fur, Best Song, Best Purr, Most Unusual. Encourage children to hold one of the pets and pretend to be the owner describing what makes his or her pet special. When each pet has been described, the awards can be handed out.

Resources
- stick-on retelling pieces
- prop board

Hunky Dory Found It

To help children retell *Hunky Dory Found It,* lean the prop board against an easel or the chalkboard, and make the stick-on retelling pieces available to the children. The story lends itself to a call-and-response type retelling where one child puts a stick-on piece on the prop board and announces who lost it, and another child picks that object up, moves it to where the dog has been placed, and says "...and Hunky Dory found it." Encourage children to recall the order in which the objects appear in the book.

INTERACTIVE LEARNING *(continued)*

Hunky Dory Found It

Ask children to volunteer to bring from home one of the objects collected by the dog in *Hunky Dory Found It:* a sock, a ball, a necktie, a book, a toy boat, and a shoe. Put all the items into a large paper grocery bag, and have children take turns pulling an object out and saying the verse from the book that goes with it. Encourage the children to remember the order in which the items are mentioned in the book.

Materials
- sock
- ball
- necktie
- book
- toy boat
- shoe
- paper grocery bag

Snow on Snow on Snow

To retell *Snow on Snow on Snow,* you can create props that children can manipulate to show story phrases such as *blankets on blankets on blankets,* or *food next to food next to food, clothes over clothes over clothes,* and so on. Draw or cut and paste the repeated story objects on each section of folded construction paper as shown. For the prop that depicts *below drifts, below drifts, below drifts,* add a fourth section with a surprise image of a shaggy dog.

Materials
- construction paper
- markers or crayons
- scissors
- paste

Games

Friendship Fun

Players: Two or More

Resources
- Friendship Fun game board
- Tokens

Preparation Name the pictures on the game board with children: *sun, game, moon, heart, mouse, garden, hat, seal, socks, mittens, girl, hook, guitar, house, mask, soap.* Have each child choose a group of tokens of one color.

Directions In turn, each player:

1. Spins the spinner and names the letter shown.

2. Finds a picture on the board with a name that begins with the sound of the indicated letter.

3. Places a token over the picture.

4. Continues playing until all the pictures are covered. The player with the most tokens on the board wins.

INTERACTIVE LEARNING *(continued)*

Additional Game Idea: Paper People Friends

Players: Two–Four

Here is an additional game idea to reinforce identification of beginning sounds.

Preparation Draw and cut out of tagboard eight paper people figures. Print one of the letters *s, m, h, g* on each of four figures. On each of the remaining figures, draw a picture whose name begins with the sound for one of the following letters: *s, m, h,* or *g.* Name the pictures with children.

Directions Players work individually or together to match paper people by pairing pictures with the letter whose sound they hear at the beginning of that picture name.

Materials
- Tagboard

Games

Resources
- Silly Pet Lotto game board
- Tokens

Silly Pet Lotto

Players: Two

Preparation Name the pictures on the spinner with children: *pig, cat, goat, monkey, seal, dog.* Each player chooses a block of letters on the game board for a playing space.

Directions In turn, each player:

1. Spins the spinner.

2. Names the picture shown on the spinner.

3. Finds on his or her block the letter with the same sound heard at the beginning of the picture name and places a token over that letter. If all squares with that letter have already been covered, the player does not put down a token.

4. Continues playing until one player covers all the letters on his or her block.

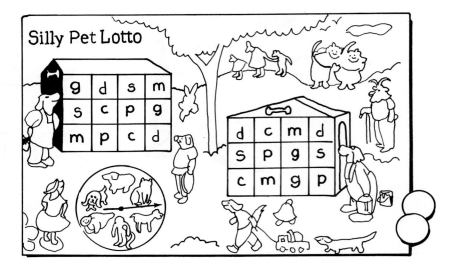

Additional Game Idea: In the Pet Shop

Players: Two

Here is an additional game idea to reinforce identification of beginning sounds.

Preparation On a large sheet of butcher paper, draw a simple pet shop with six cages. Label two cages with the letter *m,* two with the letter *p,* one with *d,* and one with *c.* Then draw or cut out from magazines the following animals: *monkey, mouse, parrot, pig, dog, cat.* Name the pictures with children. Then place the animal cards in a pile by the pet shop.

Directions In turn, each player:

1. Selects an animal card and finds in the pet shop the letter whose sound they hear at the beginning of the animal's name.

2. Places the animal in the corresponding cage in the pet shop.

3. Continues playing until all animals are placed in the pet shop.

Materials
- Butcher paper
- Old magazines

Make New Friends

Make new friends; but   keep __ the __ old, __

One   is   sil-   ver   and   the   oth-   er   gold.

Oh Where, Oh Where Has My Little Dog Gone?

Oh where, oh where has my lit- tle dog gone? Oh

where, oh where can he be? __ With his ears cut short and his

tail cut long, Oh where, oh where can he be? __

The More We Get Together

Mary Had a Little Lamb

SARAH J. HALE

Ma- ry had a   lit- tle lamb,   lit- tle lamb,   lit- tle lamb;

Ma- ry had a   lit- tle lamb, its   fleece was white as   snow.

Everywhere that Mary went,
Mary went, Mary went,
Everywhere that Mary went,
The lamb was sure to go.

It followed her to school one day,
school one day, school one day,
It followed her to school one day,
which was against the rule.

It made the children laugh and play,
laugh and play, laugh and play,
It made the children laugh and play,
to see the lamb at school.

Audio-Visual Resources

Adventure Productions
3404 Terry Lake Road
Ft. Collins, CO 80524

AIMS Media
9710 DeSoto Avenue
Chatsworth, CA
91311-4409
800-367-2467

Alfred Higgins Productions
6350 Laurel Canyon
Blvd.
N. Hollywood, CA
91606
800-766-5353

**American School
Publishers/SRA**
P.O. Box 543
Blacklick, OH
43004-0543
800-843-8855

Audio Bookshelf
R.R. #1, Box 706
Belfast, ME 04915
800-234-1713

Audio Editions
Box 6930
Auburn, CA 95604-6930
800-231-4261

Audio Partners, Inc.
Box 6930
Auburn, CA 95604-6930
800-231-4261

Bantam Doubleday Dell
1540 Broadway
New York, NY 10036
212-782-9652

Barr Films
12801 Schabarum Ave.
Irwindale, CA 97106
800-234-7878

Bullfrog Films
Box 149
Oley, PA 19547
800-543-3764

Churchill Films
12210 Nebraska Ave.
Los Angeles, CA 90025
800-334-7830

Clearvue/EAV
6465 Avondale Ave.
Chicago, IL 60631
800-253-2788

Coronet/MTI
108 Wilmot Road
Deerfield, IL 60015
800-777-8100

Creative Video Concepts
5758 SW Calusa Loop
Tualatin, OR 97062

**Dial Books for Young
Readers**
375 Hudson St.
New York, NY 10014
800-526-0275

Direct Cinema Ltd.
P.O. Box 10003
Santa Monica, CA 90410
800-525-0000

**Disney Educational
Production**
105 Terry Drive,
Suite 120
Newtown, PA 18940
800-295-5010

Encounter Video
2550 NW Usshur
Portland, OR 97210
800-677-7607

Filmic Archives
The Cinema Center
Botsford, CT 06404
800-366-1920

**Films for Humanities and
Science**
P.O. Box 2053
Princeton, NJ 08543
609-275-1400

Finley-Holiday
12607 E. Philadelphia St.
Whittier, CA 90601

Fulcrum Publishing
350 Indiana St.
Golden, CO 80401

G.K. Hall
Box 500, 100 Front St.
Riverside, NJ 08057

HarperAudio
10 East 53rd Street
New York, NY 10022
212-207-6901

Hi-Tops Video
2730 Wiltshire Blvd.
Suite 500
Santa Monica, CA 90403
213-216-7900

Houghton Mifflin/Clarion
Wayside Road
Burlington, MA 01803
800-225-3362

Idaho Public TV/Echo Films
1455 North Orchard
Boise, ID 83706
800-424-7963

Kidvidz
618 Centre St.
Newton, MA 02158
617-965-3345

L.D.M.I.
P.O. Box 1445,
St. Laurent
Quebec, Canada H4L
4Z1

Let's Create
50 Cherry Hill Rd.
Parsippany, NJ 07054

Listening Library
One Park Avenue
Old Greenwich, CT
06870
800-243-4504

Live Oak Media
P.O. Box 652
Pine Plains, NY 12567
518-398-1010

Mazon Productions
3821 Medford Circle
Northbrook, IL 60062
708-272-2824

Media Basics
Lighthouse Square
705 Boston Post Road
Guildford, CT 06437
800-542-2505

MGM/UA Home Video
1000 W. Washington
Blvd.
Culver City, CA 90232
310-280-6000

Milestone Film and Video
275 W. 96th St.,
Suite 28C
New York, NY 10025

Miramar
200 Second Ave.
Seattle, WA 98119
800-245-6472

Audio-Visual Resources *(continued)*

National Geographic
Educational Services
Washington, DC 20036
800-548-9797

The Nature Company
P.O. Box 188
Florence, KY 41022
800-227-1114

Philomel
1 Grosset Drive
Kirkwood, NY 13795
800-847-5575

Premiere Home Video
755 N. Highland
Hollywood, CA 90038
213-934-8903

Puffin Books
375 Hudson St.
New York, NY 10014

Rabbit Ears
131 Rowayton Avenue
Rowayton, CT 06853
800-800-3277

Rainbow Educational Media
170 Keyland Court
Bohemia, NY 11716
800-331-4047

Random House Media
400 Hahn Road
Westminster, MD 21157
800-733-3000

Reading Adventure
7030 Huntley Road,
Unit B
Columbus, OH 43229

Recorded Books
270 Skipjack Road
Prince Frederick,
MD 20678
800-638-1304

SelectVideo
7200 E. Dry Creek Rd.
Englewood, CO 80112
800-742-1455

Silo/Alcazar
Box 429, Dept. 318
Waterbury, VT 05676

Spoken Arts
10100 SBF Drive
Pinellas Park, FL 34666
800-126-8090

SRA
P.O. Box 543
Blacklick, OH
43004-0543
800-843-8855

Strand/VCI
3350 Ocean Park Blvd.
Santa Monica, CA 90405
800-922-3827

Taliesin Productions
558 Grove St.
Newton, MA 02162
617-332-7397

Time-Life Education
P.O. Box 85026
Richmond, VA
23285-5026
800-449-2010

Video Project
5332 College Ave.
Oakland, CA 94618
800-475-2638

Warner Home Video
4000 Warner Blvd.
Burbank, CA 91522
818-243-5020

Weston Woods
Weston, CT 06883
800-243-5020

Wilderness Video
P.O. Box 2175
Redondo Beach, CA
90278
310-539-8573

BOOKS AVAILABLE IN SPANISH
Spanish editions of English titles referred to in the Bibliography are available from the following publishers or distributors.

Bilingual Educational Services, Inc.
2514 South Grand Ave.
Los Angeles, CA
90007-9979
800-448-6032

Charlesbridge
85 Main Street
Watertown, MA 02172
617-926-5720

Children's Book Press
6400 Hollis St., Suite 4
Emeryville, CA 94608
510-655-3395

Childrens Press
5440 N. Cumberland Ave.
Chicago, IL 60656-1469
800-621-1115

Econo-Clad Books
P.O. Box 1777
Topeka, KS 66601
800-628-2410

Farrar, Straus, & Giroux
9 Union Square
New York, NY 10003
212-741-6973

Harcourt Brace
6277 Sea Harbor Drive
Orlando, FL 32887
800-225-5425

HarperCollins
10 E. 53rd Street
New York, NY 10022
717-941-1500

Holiday House
425 Madison Ave.
New York, NY 10017
212-688-0085

Kane/Miller
Box 310529
Brooklyn, NY
11231-0529
718-624-5120

Alfred A. Knopf
201 E. 50th St.
New York, NY 10022
800-638-6460

Lectorum
111 Eighth Ave.
New York, NY 10011
800-345-5946

Santillana
901 W. Walnut St.
Compton, CA 90220
800-245-8584

Simon and Schuster
866 Third Avenue
New York, NY 10022
800-223-2336

Viking
357 Hudson Street
New York, NY 10014
212-366-2000

Index

Boldface page references indicate formal strategy and skill instruction.

story clues, T17, T28, T63, T75, T86

Comprehension skills. *See* Interactive Learning; Minilessons; Skills, major; Strategies, reading.

Comprehension strategies. *See* Strategies, reading.

Computer activities. *See* Technology resources.

Concepts about print
    beginning of a sentence, **T81, T89**
    end of a written line, **T173, T189**
    end of a written word, **T141, T157**
    left to right directionality, **T41, T59**. *See also* Themes 2, 6.

Conclusions, drawing, T21, T28, T44, T52, T65, T72, T75, T115, T125, T136, T148. *See also* Inferences, making; Themes 2, 5, 12.

Consonants, beginning sounds, T47, T57, T58, T69, **T73,** T77, T78, **T87,** T136, T138, T140, **T143, T147, T155,** T167, **T169,** T175, **T177, T187,** T188. *See also* Decoding skills, consonants, beginning sounds.

Constructing meaning from text. *See* Interactive Learning.

Context
    clues, T46, T57, T78, T138, T172
    picture clues, T46, T70, T76, T78, T138, T172
    using, T46, T57, T78, T138, T172

Contractions, T70, T73, T74

Cooperative learning activities, T12, T26, T27, T36, T55, T59, T65, T85, T90, T95, T96, T97, T108, T121, T125, T139, T153, T156, T157, T160, T161, T162, T177, T185, T192, T196, T200

Cooperative reading. *See* Reading modes.

Counting, T41, T43, T51, T81, T89, T141, T170, T175

Creative dramatics
    acting out scenes, stories, and words, T27, T33, T119, T125
    demonstrating, T18, T42, T71, T147, T160
    dramatizing, T26, T27, T33, T125, T153, T192
    pantomime, T26, T54, T55, T73, T115, T159
    puppetry, T58

role-playing, T30, T55, T62, T94, T121, T131, T155, T160

Creative response. *See* Responding to literature.

Creative thinking, T27, T30, T31, T32, T33, T94, T96, T97, T161, T185

Creative writing. *See* Writing, creative.

Critical thinking, T21, T36, T40, T44, T52, T65, T81, T97, T114, T115, T154

Cross-cultural connections. *See* Multicultural activities.

Cross-curricular activities
    art, T7, T31, T55, T64, T68, T85, T92, T94, T97, T100, T125, T129, T131, T135, T153, T161, T163, T167, T197
    movement, T33, T42, T64
    health, T7, T44
    math, T7, T32, T41, T43, T96, T104, T130, T162, T170, T175, T196
    multicultural, T6, T7, T19, T49, T76, T104, T105, T117, T130, T169, T180
    music, T7, T33, T64, T96, T197
    science, T7, T23, T46, T65, T72, T75, T78, T97, T105, T116, T131, T145, T163, T171, T173, T179
    social studies, T7, T18, T25, T32, T33, T45, T65, T80, T130, T162, T196
    visual literacy, T21, T25, T38, T48, T49, T71, T72, T75, T77, T81, T122, T148, T169, T172

Cue systems. *See* Think About Words.

Cultural diversity, T7, T19, T49, T76, T104, T105, T117, T130, T169, T180. *See also* Background, building; Multicultural activities.

        initial *h*, T138
        initial *k*, **T147, T155**
        initial *p*, **T73,** T77, T78, **T87, T143**. *See also* Theme 7.
        initial *s*, T136
    phonograms
        -ig, **T79, T88**
        -it, **T139, T156**
    word attack
        context clues, T46, T57, T78, T138, T172
        contractions, T70
        dictionary, T57, T87, T155, T187, T193
        picture clues, T46, T70, T76, T78, T138, T172
        rhymes, T27, T61, T68, T79, T84, T91, T127, T134, T152, T159
        Think About Words, T46, T78, T138, T172

Details, noting, T21, T29, **T75, T86,** T92, T114, T124. *See also* Themes 1, 3, 6.

Dialogue, T26, T125

Diaries and journals. *See* Journal.

Dictionary. *See* My Big Dictionary.

Directions, following, T61, T88, T89, T157, T159

Drafting. *See* Writing skills.

Drama. *See* Creative dramatics.

E

Evaluating literature. *See* Literature, evaluating.

Evaluation. *See* Assessment options, choosing.

Extra support. *See* Individual needs, meeting.

F

Fiction, T14–T33, T34–T65, T66–T97, T112–T131, T132–T163, T166–T197

Fluency
    oral reading, T84, T152
    oral rereading, T84, T52

G

Games, H6– H9

Genre. *See* Literary genres.

Grammar and usage

adjectives, T30
contractions, T70, T73, T74
pronoun referents, T137, T147,
    T171, T172, T176
Graphic information, interpreting
charts, T94, T98, T126
Graphic organizers
chart, T17, T46, T94, T98, T126,
    T131
graph, T32, T96, T130
lists, T12, T33, T37, T57, T63, T65,
    T69, T73, T87, T91, T94, T110,
    T120, T129, T158, T163,
    T191, T195
map, T25, T33
word webs, T30, T62, T160

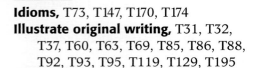

**High-Frequency Words, T38, T51,
T60, T77, T90, T137, T138, T157, T158,
T175, T190**
Home/Community Connections. *See*
Home/Community Connections
Booklet.
Home Connection, T16, T55, T57, T85,
T90, T95, T114, T121, T150, T153,
T155, T188
Home-school activities, T134, T190
Home-school communication. *See*
Home connections.
Homework. *See* Home connections.

Idioms, T73, T147, T170, T174
Illustrate original writing, T31, T32,
T37, T60, T63, T69, T85, T86, T88,
T92, T93, T95, T119, T129, T195
Illustrators
of selections
    Halpern, Shari, T4, T34, T102,
        T112
    O'Brien, Anne Sibley, T4, T14
    Rosenberry, Vera, T5, T66
    Saint James, Synthia, T103,
        T164
    Stoeke, Janet Morgan, T102,
        T103
of Watch Me Read books
    Anderson, Maja, T5
    Martin, Pedro, T103, T102
Independent reading

promoting, T92, T192
suggestions for, T92, T93, T192,
    T193
Independent reading option. *See*
Reading modes, independent
reading.
Independent writing
student-selected writing, sugges-
    tions for, T93, T193
Individual needs, meeting
challenge, T10, T26, T28, T32,
    T33, T58, T60, T62, T63, T65,
    T80, T88, T91, T95, T96,
    T108, T119, T120, T124, T127,
    T129, T143, T156, T161, T162,
    T173, T177, T180, T185
extra support, T10, T19, T20, T26,
    T28, T29, T38, T39, T41, T47,
    T56, T57, T58, T59, T60, T63,
    T73, T86, T87, T88, T89, T90,
    T94, T108, T117, T126, T127,
    T128, T137, T148, T154, T155,
    T156, T157, T158, T161, T168,
    T170, T171, T174, T179, T182,
    T186, T187, T189, T190
Students Acquiring English, T10,
    T21, T26, T27, T30, T40, T44,
    T51, T52, T54, T70, T74, T84,
    T94, T108, T115, T118, T126,
    T128, T130, T135, T138, T140,
    T147, T149, T152, T169, T172,
    T176, T178, T184, T185
Inferences, making
about characters' actions and feel-
    ings, T27, T44, T55, T176
by drawing conclusions, **T21, T28,**
    T44
by predicting, T44, T150, T168,
    T170, T176
Interactive Learning
build background, **T16, T36, T68,**
    T114, T134, T166
independent reading and writing,
    T92, T93, T192, T193
preparing to listen and write, **T16,**
    T114
shared reading and writing, **T36–**
    T37, T68» T69, T134» T135,
    T166– T167
theme, launching the, **T12, T110**
Invented spelling. *See* Spelling, tem-
    porary.

Journal, T73, T83, T119, T122, T175,
T190

Knowledge, activating prior. *See* Prior
knowledge; Background, building.

Language and usage
adjectives, T30
language games, T29, T58, T60,
    T90
See also Grammar and usage.
Language concepts and skills
alliteration, T19, T50
antonyms, T30, T119, T120, T143
humor, T142
idioms, T73, T147, T170, T174
oral language, T30, T62, T194,
    T128, T160, T194
patterns, T64, T84, T92, T134,
    T152, T184
phrases, T19, T20
repetitive pattern, T36, T54, T64
rhyme, T27, T61, T68, T79, T84,
    T91, T127, T134, T152, T159
rhythm, T36, T84
slang, T137
storytelling language, T182
word play, T29, T58, T60, T90
Language mechanics. *See* Mechanics,
language.
**Learning styles, activities employing
alternate modalities to meet individual,** T30, T54, T55, T57, T59,
T60, T63, T73, T84, T87, T88, T89,
T90, T91, T94, T97, T127, T156,
T186, T189. *See also* Individual
needs, meeting.
Limited English proficient students.
See Students acquiring English.
Linking literature
to health, T44
to math, T41, T43, T170, T175
to multicultural ideas, T19, T49,
    T76, T117, T130, T169, T180
to science, T23, T46, T72, T75,
    T78, T116, T145, T171, T173,
    T179

to social studies, T18, T25, T45,
T80
visual literacy, T21, T25, T38, T48,
T49, T71, T72, T75, T77, T81,
T122, T148, T169, T172

Listening activities
content
to audiotapes, T7, T12, T16,
T36, T59, T61, T68, T91,
T105, T159, T191
to dramatics, T18, T26, T27,
T33, T71, T119, T125,
T147, T153, T160, T192
final sounds, T117, T127
to guest speakers, T150, T162
to literature discussion, T50,
T55, T85, T100, T122,
T125, T153, T185, T197,
T200
to oral presentations, T27,
T128, T194, T200
to oral reading, T36, T47, T73,
T79, T81, T87, T88, T114,
T116, T128, T134, T143,
T150, T166, T169
to poetry, T36, T61, T134
to a read aloud, T19, T36
to rhymes, T61, T79, T91,
T159
songs, T12, T16
to teacher modeling, T18, T19,
T21, T22, T24, T41, T45,
T47, T51, T73, T75, T79,
T81, T116, T117, T118,
T120, T121, T122, T137,
T139, T141, T143, T147,
T149, T169, T173, T177,
T181
to think aloud, T18, T19, T21,
T22, T41, T45, T68, T75,
T79, T81, T116, T118,
T121, T122, T141, T166
purpose
for beginning sounds, T19,
T29, T47, T50, T57, T58,
T73, T77, T87, T147, T155,
T169, T177, T187
for enjoyment, T18, T26, T27,
T33, T71, T119, T125,
T147, T153, T160, T192
to analyze and evaluate, T28,
T154, T166, T173, T181,
T186

to compare sounds, T19, T29,
T47, T50, T57, T58, T73,
T77, T87, T117, T127, T147,
T155, T169, T177, T187
to follow directions, T61, T88,
T89, T157, T159
to gain information, T131,
T143, T171, T173, T179
to patterns, T61
to recall information and
details, T116, T128, T143,
T149, T154, T181, T186
to reread, T21, T26, T54, T78,
T84, T89, T91, T92, T94,
T124, T152, T159, T174,
T192
for sharing, T12, T17, T18, T27,
T32, T36, T50, T68, T85,
T86, T89, T93, T96, T100,
T110, T114, T122, T125,
T127, T129, T134, T158,
T166, T188, T194, T197,
T200

Literary appreciation, T55, T85, T153,
T185, T192. *See also* Interactive
Learning; Literary devices.

Literary devices
alliteration, T19
detail, use of, T21, T29, T47, T75,
T86, T92, T114, T124
dialogue, T26, T125
humor, T142
patterns, T64, T84, T92, T134,
T152, T184
phrases, T19, T20
point of view, T26, T185
repetitive pattern, T36, T54, T64
rhyme, T27, T61, T68, T79, T84,
T91, T127, T134, T152, T159
rhythm, T36, T84
storytelling language, T182

Literary genres
fiction, T14–T33, T34–T65,
T66–T97, T112–T131,
T132–T163, T166–T197
poetry, T36, T114, T134, T157,
T166

Literary skills
character. *See* Character(s).
poetic devices, T36, T114, T134,
T157, T166
setting, T86, T93
story elements, T24, T50, T186

Literature
celebrating, T100, T200
comparing, T55, T85, T100, T153,
T200
discussion, T50, T55, T85, T100,
T122, T125, T153, T185, T197,
T200
evaluating, T50, T55, T85, T100,
T122, T125, T153, T200
linking, T55, T85, T100, T153,
T197, T200
responding to. *See* Responding to
literature.

Little Big Book PLUS
Hunky Dory Found It, by Katie
Evans, T193
Snow on Snow on Snow, by
Cheryl Chapman, T193
Together, by George Ella Lyon,
T93
*What Shall We Do When We All
Go Out?* text adapted by
Philip H. Bailey, T93

M

Maps
creating, T33
using, T25

Mathematics activities. *See* Cross-
curricular activities.

Meaning, constructing from text. *See*
Interactive Learning; Skills,
major; Strategies, reading.

Mechanics, language
capitalization
first word of sentence, T81
proper names, T135
punctuation
question mark, T39

Meeting individual needs. *See*
Individual needs, meeting.

Metacognition. *See* Strategies,
reading; Think Aloud.

Minilessons
concepts about print, **T41, T81,
T173**
comprehension, **T21, T45, T75,
T149, T181**
High-Frequency Words, **T51, T77,
T137**
phonemic awareness, **T19, T117**
phonics/decoding, **T47, T73, T139,**

T143, T147, T169
Modeling, teacher, T18, T19, T21, T22, T24, T41, T45, T47, T51, T73, T75, T79, T81, T116, T117, T118, T120, T121, T122, T137, T139, T141, T143, T147, T149, T169, T173, T177, T181
Monitoring comprehension option. *See* Strategies, reading.
Multi-age classroom, T9, T107
Multicultural activities/information
    animal sounds in other cultures, T180
    bicycles in other cultures, T19
    breakfast food in other cultures, T169
    chariot racing, T76
    hide-and-seek games, T49
    Japanese pets, T117
    pets in other cultures, T130
My Big Dictionary, T57, T87, T155, T187, T193

N

Narrative text, T14–T33, T34–T65, T66–T97, T112–T131, T132–T163, T166–T197

O

Oral
    choices for oral language, T30, T62, T194, T128, T160, T194
    composition. *See* Speaking activities.
    language, T30, T62, T194, T128, T160, T194. *See* Speaking activities.
    presentation, T27, T128, T194, T200
    reading, T54, T59, T60, T84, T90, T91, T153. *See* Rereading.
    summary, T24, T50, T73, T82, T120, T142

P

Paired learning, T30, T54, T55, T57, T59, T60, T63, T73, T84, T87, T88, T89, T90, T91, T94, T97, T127, T156, T186, T189
Parent involvement. *See* Home Connection.

Peer interaction. *See* Cooperative learning activities; Learning styles: paired learning.
Personal response, T16, T36, T68, T114, T125, T134, T153, T167, T185
    Phonemic awareness
    recognizes the first sound of a spoken word, **T19, T29**
    recognizes the last sounds of a spoken words, **T117, T127**
Phonics. *See* Decoding skills.
Pluralism. *See* Cultural diversity.
Poetry
    discussion, T36, T114, T134, T157, T166
    introducing, reading, responding to, T36, T114, T134, T157, T166
    in Teacher's Book
        "First Snow," T166
        "In Downtown Philadelphia," T134, T157
        "My Bird is Small," T114
        "With a Friend," T36
    Point of view, T26
Predictions, making
    from previewing, T16, T36, T93, T114, T134, T166, T192
    while reading, T44, T150, T169, T170, T176
Previewing
    cover, T16, T68, T93, T114, T134, T166, T192
    illustrations, T16, T36, T68, T93, T114, T134, T166, T192
    title, T16, T36, T68, T93, T114, T134, T166, T192
Prewriting. *See* Writing skills.
Prior knowledge, T36, T68, T70, T75, T78, T122, T166, T176
Problem/solution, T17
Publishing. *See* Writing skills.
Punctuation. *See* Mechanics, language.
Purpose setting for reading, T18, T38, T70, T116, T136, T168

Q

Questions, generating, T62, T70, T168, T191

R

Read Aloud books
    I Have a Pet! by Shari Halpern, T102, T112–T131
    Jamaica's Find by Juanita Havill, T14–T33
Reading across the curriculum
    art, T7, T31, T55, T64, T68, T85, T92, T94, T97, T100, T125, T129, T131, T135, T153, T161, T163, T167, T197
    movement, T33, T42, T64
    health, T7, T44
    math, T7, T32, T41, T43, T96, T104, T130, T162, T170, T175, T196
    multicultural, T6, T7, T19, T49, T76, T104, T105, T117, T130, T169, T180
    music, T7, T33, T64, T96, T197
    science, T7, T23, T46, T65, T72, T75, T78, T97, T105, T116, T131, T145, T163, T171, T173, T179
    social studies, T7, T18, T25, T32, T33, T45, T65, T80, T130, T162, T196
    visual literacy, T21, T25, T38, T48, T49, T71, T72, T75, T77, T81, T122, T148, T169, T172
Reading log, T193
Reading modes
    choral reading, T54
    cooperative reading, T36, T54, T68, T84, T92, T134, T166, T184
    echo reading, T84, T152
    independent reading, T61, T92 T192
    oral reading, T54, T59, T60, T84, T90, T91, T153
    shared reading, T36, T68, T134, T166
Reading strategies. *See* Strategies, reading.
Reference and study skills. *See* Study skills.
Rereading
    comprehension, T17, T21, T26, T28, T38, T45, T54, T56, T59, T78, T84, T86, T89, T94, T114, T124, T136, T149, T152, T154,

T192
retelling, T16, T24, T26, T50,
T55, T56, T82, T85, T114,
T124, T153, T154, T167,
T185, T186
rhyme, T127
sentences, T51, T60, T69, T88,
T90, T135, T156, T190
singing, T12, T16, T36, T37,
T54, T55, T64, T68, T110,
T194, T197
storytelling, T56
summary, T24, T50, T73, T82,
T120, T142
purpose
analyzing/evaluating litera-
ture, T22, T27, T28, T38,
T40, T55, T85, T100
contributing information, T16,
T19, T21, T25, T28, T32,
T36, T38, T44, T47, T80,
T95, T100, T118, T120,
T126, T179, T180, T182,
T187, T191
giving opinions, T21, T22, T27,
T28, T32, T40, T48, T50,
T62, T68, T72, T76, T80,
T85, T92, T100, T114,
T116, T125, T150, T182,
T184, T200
role-play, T30, T55, T62, T94,
T121, T131, T155, T160
See also Creative dramatics;
Oral, reading.
Speech, parts of. *See also* Grammar
and usage; Language and usage.
Spelling
conventional, T51, T63, T83, T88,
T156, T167
temporary, T51, T57, T84, T88,
T89, T155, T187, T193
words with
-ig, T88
-it, T139, T156
See also Decoding skills,
phonograms.
Story elements/story structure
beginning, T24, T50, T186
end, T24, T50, T186
middle, T 24, T50, T186
setting, T86, T93
Storytelling, T56
Storytelling/retelling, props, T85,

T125, T153, T185, H2–H5
Strategic reading. *See* Strategies,
reading; Vocabulary, During
reading.
Strategies, reading
evaluate, T22, T38, T48, T50, T72,
T76, T82, T118, T122, T142,
T148, T150, T176, T182
monitor, T18, T40, T44, T52, T70,
T116, T118, T136, T144, T146,
T168, T174, T180
predict/infer, T150, T168, T170,
T176
self-question, T18, T40, T44, T70,
T116, T118, T136
summarize, T24, T50, T76, T82,
T120, T142
Think About Words, T20, T46,
T78, T138, T172
Student self-assessment. *See*
Assessment: Self-assessment; Self-
assessment.
**Students acquiring English, activities
especially helpful for**
expressions/idioms, T138, T169
key concepts, T10, T26, T27, T40,
T94, T108, T126, T149, T152
paired/group learning, T54, T84,
T94, T115, T128, T135, T138,
T184, T185
primary language, T128
resource to class, T10, T21, T44,
T51, T52, T108, T130
word meanings, T10, T30, T40,
T70, T74, T108, T118, T140,
T147, T172, T176, T178
Study skills
graphic sources
graph, T32, T96, T130
reference sources
dictionary, T57, T87, T155,
T187, T193
magazines, using, T12, T187
maps, using, T25
study strategies
directions, following, T61,
T88, T89, T157, T159
Study strategies. *See* Skills, major;
Strategies, reading; Study skills.
Summarizing
oral summaries, T24, T50, T73,
T82, T120, T142

Synonyms, T40, T173, T177, T180

T

Teaching across the curriculum. *See*
Content areas, reading in the; Cross-
curricular activities.
Teaching and management
managing assessment, T11, T99,
T109, T199
managing instruction, T10, T108
special needs of students, meeting.
See Individual needs, meeting.
teaching tips, T93, T193
Tear-and-Take stories, T90, T190
Technology resources
Internet, Houghton Mifflin, T7,
T12, T15, T35, T67, T100,
T105, T110, T113, T133, T165,
T200
Theme, celebrating, T100, T200
Theme concepts, T9, T100, T200
Theme, launching the, T12, T110
Theme projects, T12, T100, T110,
T200
Theme
Let's Be Friends, T12–T100
Playful Pets, T110–T200
Think About Words
picture clues, T46, T78, T138,
T172
sounds for letters, T46, T78, T138,
T172
what makes sense, T46, T78,
T138, T172
Think Aloud, T18, T19, T21, T22, T41,
T45, T68, T75, T79, T81, T116,
T118, T121, T122, T141, T166
Thinking
creatively. *See* Creative thinking.
critically. *See* Critical thinking.

U

Usage. *See* Language and usage.

V

Videotapes, T7, T105
Viewing
environment, T33
illustrations, T16, T117, T21, T23,
T24, T25, T28, T32, T38, T45,
T46, T48, T49, T68, T70, T71,